*Life Woven with Song*

VOLUME 41

*Sun Tracks*
An American Indian Literary Series

SERIES EDITOR
Ofelia Zepeda

EDITORIAL COMMITTEE
Vine Deloria, Jr.
Larry Evers
Joy Harjo
Geary Hobson
N. Scott Momaday
Irvin Morris
Simon J. Ortiz
Emory Sekaquaptewa
Leslie Marmon Silko
Luci Tapahonso

# Life Woven with Song

NORA MARKS DAUENHAUER

The University of Arizona Press    Tucson

The University of Arizona Press
© 2000 by Nora Marks Dauenhauer

www.uapress.arizona.edu

Library of Congress Cataloging-in-Publication Data
Dauenhauer, Nora.
    Life woven with song / Nora Marks Dauenhauer.
        p.  cm. — (Sun tracks ; v. 41)
    ISBN 0-8165-2005-4 (alk. paper)
    ISBN 0-8165-2006-2 (pbk. : alk. paper)
    1. Tlingit Indians—Literary collections. 2. Indians of North America—
Alaska—Literary collections. 3. Indians of North America—Alaska. 4. Tlingit
Indians. I. Title. II. Series.
    PS501.S85 vol. 41    810.8'08972—dc21    [PS3554.A83]    99-006845

Publication of this book is made possible in part by the proceeds of a
permanent endowment created with the assistance of a Challenge Grant
from the National Endowment for the Humanities, a federal agency.

Manufactured in the United States of America on acid-free,
archival-quality paper.

13   12   11   10   09   08     7   6   5   4   3   2

*To my loving husband*

# Contents

# Figures

# *Preface*

In this book are snippets of me and my family in the contexts in which we worked—work we enjoyed doing and work we did to keep alive. There are memories of my father trolling, trolling with his entire family, or the entire family in dryfish camp; of making a living in a cash economy by working in canneries; of my grandfather when he could no longer see; of my Auntie Jennie when she started to train me to be a grandmother; of a favorite basketball player; and of Tlingit elders. Memories of seasons, and of stories that were told at many places: in clan houses, in hunting and trapping camps.

Not all of the memories are of childhood. Many of my poems are of new images and memories of my grandchildren. I think that everyone is left with memories of their heritage, and these memories continue to teach us. They are a gift that keeps giving. In a way, this is what my writing is, my poems, plays, and prose. My family left me these images and memories, and I would like to keep them alive.

Most of the memories recalled here are happy ones. Where the images are neutral, negative, or discouraging, I like to think that they reflect our ability to continue as individuals, as a family, as a community, as a people.

People often ask me about my work, so I'll answer some of the most common questions here, anticipating that readers may be wondering about these things. I'd like to say a few words here about the style and themes of my poetry and prose (comments on the plays are presented as a separate introduction to that section of the book). In gathering together my work of many years for this collection, it was interesting for me to see several themes unfold. There are the recurring themes of food and land, salmon and the rain forest. The treatment may be serious or silly (as in the Raven plays), but the themes are there. In editing for this collection, I discovered how the themes are explored from different perspectives (from my point of view as a child, as a mother, as a grandmother) and through different literary forms (as poems, stories, plays, and autobiographical pieces). I guess they are all ultimately autobiographical. I hope the separate pieces come together for readers to form a larger cultural and literary landscape.

Readers' reactions to my story "Egg Boat" vary. Some people like it a lot, others not at all. In "Egg Boat" and in some of the other prose pieces, I am trying to handle character, conflict, and dialogue in a different way. I am bothered by the "endless chatter" of TV sitcoms and of much children's literature. I am trying for a more quiet "inner dialogue," and for conflict not among the characters, but within the individual, as the individual finds himself or herself in the natural and cultural environment, in this case me as a twelve-year-old girl fishing the North Pacific for the first time alone. As one Tlingit high school girl recently said in describing her first experience in a traditional fish camp with elders, designed to complement the analytical elements of the school science curriculum, "I learned to find courage in myself, and I learned to trust others."

Now, a word about the setting. The work in this collection is mostly about home, but some of it is inspired by places I visit, whether elsewhere in Alaska, elsewhere in the United States, or elsewhere in the world. What's home for me may be exotic to others. Like most Tlingit Indians, I live in southeast Alaska, in the middle of the largest temperate rain forest in the world, extending from northern California to Kodiak Island. Our part of this is an archipelago about the same size and shape as Florida. Few towns are connected by roads, so we travel by air, boat, and state ferry. Igloos and dogsleds are images from farther north in Alaska. We are the people of totem poles, Chilkat blankets, carved wooden hats and helmets, bentwood boxes, oceangoing canoes, and other products of the coastal rain forest. Our lives have traditionally been oriented toward beaches and boats. Once, on the Tohono O'odham reservation in the Sonoran Desert of southern Arizona, I asked the kids how many of them had been in a boat. Not one. How about horses? All the hands shot up! Most of our kids have never seen or ridden a real horse. My first time on horseback was a trail ride on the beach at Neah Bay led by a teenage Makah girl. Native Americans are not all the same. Because some of the lifestyle and language of southeast Alaska may not be familiar to readers elsewhere, I have included a glossary at the end.

Finally, I would like to thank Ofelia Zepeda, Patti Hartmann, and the other editors at Sun Tracks and the University of Arizona Press for their faith in this book and for their patience during its delivery. Thanks also to my husband, Dick, who word-processed the manuscript and offered encouragement and advice along the way. He is also the photographer for the photos in this book that are not otherwise credited.

# *Part One*

## PROSE

# Some Slices of Salmon

The first European and Euro-American explorers to southeast Alaska found us Tlingits in various places drying salmon. We Tlingit have always been eating salmon.

There are five species of salmon in Alaska: king, or Chinook, which is the largest; sockeye, or red; coho, or silver; chum, or dog salmon; and humpy (humpback), or pink. Salmon eggs hatch in fresh water; salmon spend most of their developing years in salt water and return to their home stream during the summer months to spawn and die. During this phase, their color and shape change dramatically.

Not only have we always used salmon as our main diet, and not only has it been the mainstay of our subsistence and commercial economies, but the different varieties of salmon are a part of our social structure and ethnic identity as well. Beyond the physical use of salmon as food, salmon have symbolic and totemic value. Many clans have salmon as their crest. My clan is called Lukaax̱.ádi in Tlingit; the name derives from a salmon river in Duncan Canal near Petersburg, Alaska. Our principal emblem is the sockeye or red salmon.

The L'uknax̱.ádi clan derives its Tlingit name from another place of origin, related to the Tlingit word for coho salmon, which is their principal crest. The L'eineidí clan has the dog salmon as its crest, and the Kwaashk'ikwaan use the humpy or humpback salmon. Increasingly, most Tlingit clans are becoming known by the English names of their principal crest animal; thus the above-mentioned groups are commonly called Sockeye Clan, Coho Clan, Dog Salmon Clan, and so on.

Tlingit clans historically owned areas of economic production that were most often also places of importance in the Tlingit spiritual geography. Many of these places are important salmon rivers. For example, my clan, the Lukaax̱.ádi or Sockeye, owned part of the Alsek River, and we have among our clan crests Heen Kwéiyi, known in English as Gateway Knob, where the salmon migrate up the Alsek River. Our clan also traditionally owned Chilkoot Lake and Chilkoot River, near Haines.

This enduring relationship between the Tlingit people, the fish and animals, and the land, and the connection of all of these to our social structure, took many generations to evolve. The personal experiences of ancestors with the various forms of life and landscape are passed down in the oral tradition and visual art of each clan. In this way, the education of the future stewards of a clan crest or tribal lands traditionally took place, informing the upcoming generation how to handle crests properly, when to handle them, who should handle them, and how to talk about them. Traditionally minded Tlingit people wear and otherwise display their clan crests during ceremonies such as memorials for the departed. The crest designs alluding to the events are inscribed or painted on, carved, sewn, or woven as ceremonial objects. Our crest art objects function as our ancestors, identifying us as being their descendants. This is the way I was raised as we moved from place to place in a very conservative, Tlingit-speaking extended family, following the subsistence lifestyle.

Images of salmon are important throughout Tlingit and other Alaska Native oral tradition. In her telling of "The Glacier Bay History," the late Susie James focused on the salmon run as a central image of the "myth of eternal return," that when people live in harmony with the cosmos, the salmon return in abundance, and the land provides. In another story, probably very ancient, and popular in Tsimshian and Haida oral literature as well as Tlingit (and claimed by all three groups as a clan crest), a young boy rejects the dryfish his mother offers him because part of it is moldy. This offends the salmon people, and as part of the child's education, he is taken or "captured" by the salmon people. He eventually returns home with the salmon run, is recognized by his people (usually because the necklace he always wore was now around a salmon neck), is restored to human form, and becomes a shaman and cultural mediator between humans and the salmon. This story is well documented in the turn-of-the-century collections by Franz Boas and John Swanton. In Tlingit tradition, this story belongs to the Kiks.ádi clan of Sitka. The Koyukon Athapaskan people of interior Alaska have a wonderful riddle: We come upstream in red canoes. The answer, of course, is salmon.

The crest objects may also be considered deeds to land in traditional use and ownership by the group using the crest. In a striking example of this, our late clan leader from Haines wore his Chilkat robe with the sockeye salmon design as evidence in a court dispute over our clan's ownership of the land on which our clan house is situated. "We wear our history," he testified.

With the arrival of Euro-Americans, many Tlingit and other Alaska Native people were separated from their land and resource base. For example, many canneries were built at the mouth of salmon streams traditionally claimed by Tlingit clans and used for subsistence fishing. Tlingit people historically practiced subsistence hunting, fishing, and logging without dominating or destroying the natural resource. Traditional Tlingit fish traps were woven and could be hand-carried. In contrast, the canneries built barge-sized fish traps that were anchored along the migration routes, intercepting thousands of salmon on their way to spawn. Entire salmon runs were depleted by fish traps and by logging practices that ruined their habitat. The Tlingit protested fish traps and the usurping of their land, but to little avail. In 1953 President Eisenhower declared the fishing communities of southeast Alaska a disaster area. Fish traps were outlawed only in 1959, with the coming of Alaska statehood. The controversy over subsistence fishing continues to rage.

As with land, subsistence is at the very core of our ethnic identity and tribal existence. The importance of salmon goes beyond the question of calories. It is part of our identity. We need salmon to continue as physically, mentally, and spiritually healthy people.

The period described in my two childhood pieces is from the mid-1930s to the early 1940s. Although my father eagerly embraced new technology, his values and those of the extended family were very conservative. He was the first to get a gas or diesel engine, but we were among the last families who still followed a traditional subsistence lifestyle and who still spoke only Tlingit at home. (I was eight years old before I started school and first heard English.) This was still before freezers. We preserved salmon in dry-fish camp the way Tlingits had been doing it presumably forever. Our family lived on a boat. Before World War II, we wintered in tents at Graves Harbor and other sites on the outer Pacific coast of what is now Glacier Bay National Park. It was a moving experience in August 1997 to revisit the places of my childhood with a Park Service archaeologist, and to find the remains of tentsites and workshops of more than fifty years ago. The war and truant officers gradually brought this era to a close. But the memories remain.

Having first looked at salmon in a more conceptual, adult, academic, and anthropological way, I now invite you to share in other slices of salmon from different points of view: childhood memories of trolling for king salmon; memories of our traditional dryfish camp; a short story; some modern plays based on old and outrageous Raven stories; and all of this spiced with poetry.


## TROLLING

I woke to something hitting the deck outside. It sounded like a salmon slamming its tail on the deck. Before long there was another of the same noise, then another, and another. Wow! My father must be filling up the fish bin by his girdies, and the salmon are still bouncing.

I wanted to see what was happening, so I quickly jumped out of my bunk and dressed. On my rush through the galley I grabbed a piece of bread for breakfast and started up the stairs to the back deck. I could see that it was a clear day, with a lot of sky.

When my father came into view, he was busy. He looked like he was tangled in a bundle of steel, and at the same time he looked like he was juggling salmon. In front of him were flipping salmon everywhere. The sounds were incredible: the flipping wires, the musical sound of the spoons, the gaff slamming salmon. In my father's right hand was the gaff hook, which doubled as a club for the salmon. He was hooking the salmon with his right hand as he pulled his power girdy on with his left. The deck was alive with flipping salmon. My father was trying to keep them from sliding overboard. All the while, he was looking for which of the four trolling poles had salmon on, or which of the salmon on the poles should be pulled up next.

They were king salmon! (Also called Chinook.) Of all salmon, the most beautiful is the king. When freshly caught it's very light silvery and dark silver, with iridescent pink and blue in the scales, and with black dots along the back and side. The head is mostly black inside the mouth. When they're caught and flipping, they flash like a pouring out of multicolored jewels. They curl every which way. They twist in crescent shapes like silver bracelets inlaid or studded with jewels.

After he had let the line back down again, with its hooks and shining spoons, he yelled, "Nora! Get a knife and start cleaning the salmon! Get the ones that aren't flipping!"

"What fun!" I thought. I ran downstairs and tried to get a sharp knife. I found one and ran back on deck. I started cleaning as fast as I could.

My father said, "Let me see. Gills first, then the belly. Take your time, but do a good job. Clean them good. Remember, this fish buyer checks over how they look inside."

As he said this, my two brothers, Alex and Raymond, came on deck, still yawning from a heavy sleep. Pop said, "You guys start cleaning the salmon with your sister. One of you wash them and cover them with a gunnysack. Put the clean salmon in the salmon

A fishing boat rigged to troll for salmon.

box. Lay them out so that we can put a lot in. Wash the box with fresh water!" He meant seawater. The gulls flying over us were going crazy in anticipation.

We continued in this vein for a while, then the frenzy started slowing down. My father was smiling the whole day. We didn't stop, even after the biting frenzy slowed to almost nothing. The noise of the gulls was very loud above the noise of the engine.

While the salmon were really biting, Mom poked her head out from time to time. She was at the wheel all during the good fishing. She circled back each time she thought she had passed the school of salmon.

Only after Pop sold the salmon did we kids find out that what we had experienced that day was once-in-a-lifetime luck. My father was at the right place at the right time and came on a migrating school of salmon. It was great for all of us who experienced it. We were very happy.

All the time we were busy we were wishing for Grandma Eliza and Auntie Anny, whom we had left at our home port to look for natural foods from the forest and beaches, so they didn't witness the fishing frenzy.

It was my first experience as a salmon cleaner. I have never again seen a school of salmon bite like that.


DRYFISH CAMP

Pop had anchored the *New Anny* by the coho salmon stream where we traveled every year to gather our winter supply of fish for the entire extended family. It was at the head of a deep inlet off of Icy Strait, not too far from Glacier Bay. Everyone was excited and talking all at once.

"Nás'k handid áwé yánzgaa kugei̱x," someone was saying. "Three hundred is usually enough."

Pop was cooking, usually salmon and its various parts, possibly the head. Auntie Anny was saying, "I'll help gather the salmon."

Pop said, "I wish she would stay on board and not come along.

We really don't have much room on the sealing boat. It's tippy." He more or less mumbled it, so Auntie didn't hear him. She was all ready to go.

Grandma Eliza always managed to convince her sons (Jim, John, and Willie) to get at least three hundred salmon for drying in the fall of every year. Over the years her sons had built four smokehouses in three different places for her and the family. An older and now a newer one were near the entrance of the inlet where we were anchored. The third smokehouse was at another protected cove nearby and was used for drying halibut in spring. At the start of World War II, when travel to the Pacific Ocean end of Icy Strait was restricted, they built the fourth smokehouse at another natural harbor at the inland end of Icy Strait. This became our last stop before winter. But that's another story.

We, the children on board the *New Anny*, were keeping our eyes on the river where our father and uncles had gone to get salmon. We no sooner looked when we would be looking again. Then what looked like a drift log floated out of the mouth of the river. Another followed, then a third.

As they got closer, the logs looked as if their branches were tipping ever so slightly. We thought the branches dipped like oars. Then we saw they were oars that looked like branches. It moved so slowly. It was one of the sealing boats they had filled almost to the brim with salmon. They were so low in the water that at first they looked like logs. They were rowing so slowly so the salmon wouldn't shift in the boat and tip it over. When they were closer out in the bay, you could almost see the shapes of the people in the boats.

We watched them coming all the way to the side of the *New Anny*. When they got near to us, we could see they had a lot of salmon. We kids were happy. My little brothers were jumping for joy. The salmon were all water marked with red—mostly cohoes and chums. The chums were green with some red and black circles on their bodies. According to tradition, a brown bear is said to have put these marks on them; they are the claw marks of a brown bear.

All of the salmon heads were gray and black; they were beautiful. We could see all the salmon in the rowboats as they got next to our bigger boat.

My father said, "Start boiling water for boiled salmon!" One of the boys ran down to the galley to start the boiling water. My father had his favorite treat already soaking in cold water—the finest coho heads and tails, to be eaten raw.

We children watched as they unloaded their catch. The other boats rowed up to the *New Anny*. They had a lot of salmon but not quite enough. They had to go back and get more.

When I was older, I got to share in what happened on shore. We always went to get our salmon for smoking from there. My father set the net by going upriver from us with my brother Alex in a rowboat. As they started off, my brother threw the seine overboard while my father yelled "Let 'er go!" and rowed, smiling, toward the opposite shore. Almost crossing the river, he turned toward us on the beach downstream from where he had started out.

When he was close and Alex was laughing and almost out of net, we waited to catch him on the shore. When he hit the beach, we grabbed the bowline and someone grabbed the end of the lead line and the cork line of the net, and we started pulling in the net. The corks on the net were dancing on the river. We knew this meant there were salmon in there.

While we were pulling up the net—my brothers, Alex and Raymond; my father, Willie; and our deckhand, Eddy Jackson—we could begin to see the salmon in the net. Some of the cohoes were red; others were still silver. The chum or dog salmon were green, black, and red. Some of us were shouting and having a great time.

We worked fast. You have to when you do this kind of work. So as we pulled the net full of salmon onto the beach, we grabbed them and threw them up where they wouldn't flutter into the river again and swim away. The entire bank of the river was aflutter with silver, red, green, and black. The band where the seine lay was like a giant macramé necklace—but with diamonds, emeralds, and rubies. It was a sight to see.

My Auntie Anny had a club in her hand to hit the nose of the salmon with. This is how we caught our salmon in the river. We set our net over and over until we had enough fish for the winter.

When we had enough fish on board, Pop would weigh anchor, and the family moved with the catch to the smokehouse site, where we smoked and dried the salmon. We'd stay there a month or so—for as long as it took to prepare the food for winter.

When we got to dryfish camp it was almost night. We could hear an owl hooting in the woods. We had dinner and sleep.

The next day was preparation for butchering salmon. The men lined up two sealing boats on the beach during the morning high tide and filled them half up with seawater.

After sharpening their knives, they were ready. They butchered by cutting the head off and gutting them. We split the salmon down along one side of the backbone, cutting through the small, riblike bones but not through the skin. One side of the split salmon has the tail, which is then broken but not cut away.

Every one of the adults was butchering salmon and putting them in the boats full of salt water. Once in a while they stirred the water. Anyone who wasn't butchering was carrying a salmon or two in each hand to go into the smokehouse, where they were hung, flesh side in, over sticks that reached from wall to wall.

Some of the men made tables out of boards or good-sized boxes. Grandma sat at the edge of the beach rye grass. She had toppled some over and was using the bunches as a pad to cut her salmon on. This was her layer of protection against sand and gravel. She always used what was already available in the natural environment. She didn't need very much equipment—just her knife and gloves. Grandma always moved slowly, but she was steady and she never quit!

As they butchered they saved the heads, especially the large ones. They split these. At low tide, the men dug a large pit and lined it with skunk cabbage. Then they put a bunch of innards from the salmon in it. On top of this they put the salmon heads.

Nora's daughters Leonora and Carmela slicing salmon for the smokehouse.

They kept on adding the innards and layering the heads, spread open. This is how we make k'ínk'—fermented fish heads. There are four tides a day: two high and two low. The rising and falling tide rinses and flushes the fish heads with natural brine. In about two weeks they are ready to eat. In this way, we were able to fill the smokehouse with fish and the pit on the beach with salmon heads.

While we smoked the salmon, our father trolled for king salmon. When he trolled and the weather was too bad for fish buyers to come by, or if it was too far for him to go in the bad weather, he salted the salmon in kegs for winter use.

Some of the women with older children went berry picking while we smoked the salmon. After three or four days of smoking salmon and picking berries, the entire family began splitting the hanging salmon for the second phase of drying, being careful not to mash or split the flesh. The men hand the fish down from the

Nora preparing thinly sliced salmon for the smokehouse.

drying racks to the women, who are splitting the salmon. The women carefully slice them and fillet for strips. This is one of the tastiest parts of dried salmon, called in Tlingit "at yuwaa x̲'éeshi."

For lunch or dinner we cooked half-smoked fish tails either on barbecue sticks or by boiling. When done, you can dip them into seal oil. Tasty! This is very delicious after berry picking, especially with fresh berries for dessert. The berries included blueberries, huckleberries, lowbush cranberries, and elderberries. Elderberries must be cooked. Some of the time we got fresh fruit, such as watermelon or cantaloupe, from the fish buyers, though not too much. Sometimes we had salmon eggs with seaweed for lunch or dinner.

When the salmon were coated with smoke after being sliced, we often had some of them for dinner, especially those that were cracked or mashed by accident. The half-dried salmon is called "náayadi" in Tlingit. We also had fresh king salmon that Papa caught on his powerboat.

We stayed almost a month smoking the salmon. Approximately a week before they are completely dry, all of the salmon are skewered on sticks that hold them up by their side bones. They are raised to a higher level of the smokehouse. At this time, we use larger fires, but we have to be careful not to make the fire too big. The family still remembers and talks about how Uncle Jimmy once put so much wood on the smokehouse fire that he nearly burned the smokehouse down. But that's another story.

When all the salmon were smoked, we packed up, broke camp, and headed to Hoonah or Juneau for the winter. The three-hundred-plus salmon were going to be our main diet all winter. The dryfish was divided four ways: Grandma, Grandpa, and Auntie Anny; our family—Willie and Emma Marks and us kids; and Uncle Jim, Auntie Jennie, and our cousin, Horace; Uncle John, Auntie Mary, and their daughter, Elizabeth. For each family, this amounted to about seventy-five salmon plus the by-products such as strips from the second splitting, salmon tails that will be used until gone, and salmon eggs—some in berry pudding already, and

Slices of smoked salmon.

some fermenting in kegs. The fermented heads were all eaten up directly from the pit, where the daily cycle of high and low tides had washed and rinsed them.

Another delicacy we put up at the end of dryfish camp was fermented salmon eggs packed in seal stomachs along with dried salmon strips. The eggs are mashed and pounded and pushed into the stomach, and the dried strips are also pushed in. Whenever seals were shot and butchered, the stomachs were inflated and dried and set aside for when it was time to use them. This was a kind of Tlingit "power bar" of my childhood, and I often get nostalgic for it.

My fondest memories of dryfish camp are of the site at the eastern end of Icy Strait. The site was selected for its multiple uses. Not only was it near the source of fish from streams or trolling, but berries were abundant and the hunting was good. We could leave for our winter village not only with dryfish and saltfish, and fermented fish eggs, but also with deer meat and berries. The berries! Sometimes Pop would get angry with the women, grumbling, "Too many berries!" as he tried to find a place to put them on the boat, but in the winter they tasted so good as dessert after eating the salmon dryfish!

# Egg Boat

*I*n the fall of every year, K̲eixwnéi and her family went trolling for coho salmon. The season for trolling usually opened in midsummer, and the run became intense toward the end of the cannery season when the whole family went to the cannery to earn their money. Her father seined for the canning company while her Auntie Anny and sometimes her mother worked processing the catch from the salmon seiners. Because the family worked for the cannery, they lived the summer season in the company houses.

Some years the catch of salmon seiners began to decrease before the seining season came to an end, but around this time coho trolling began to pick up. In order to get in on the favorable runs when the salmon began to migrate to the rivers for spawning, trollers had to be ready.

This was one of the times they were going to go fishing early. Her father had observed on their last trip that there were signs of coho, but he wasn't catching too much salmon in his seine. So he stripped his seine off the boat and began to replace it with trolling gear.

While Pop prepared the gas boat for trolling, the rest of the family packed their belongings from the company houses and transferred them to the boat. Everyone helped get everything aboard.

Mom packed things from their house, and Grandma and Auntie packed things from theirs. K̲eixwnéi and her younger brothers and sisters carried things they could carry easily, and the little ones carried things like pots and pans. In this way everyone worked.

The older boys were big enough to help their father get the

boat gassed up and get fresh water for the trips. So they had plenty to do, too, besides helping Grandma and Auntie pack their belongings down to the boat.

When the *New Anny* was finally ready, they left port in the early afternoon and headed toward Point Adolfus. The tide was going out, and this was the right current to catch, which would carry them quickest to their destination.

It was on a similar tide the previous year while they were coming to Hoonah from Cape Spencer that Ḵeixwnéi's father spotted a little square-ended rowboat floating on the Icy Strait's water. He picked it up and he and the boys put it on the deck of the boat. They had it on deck when they stopped in Hoonah. Everyone saw it and commented on what a nice boat it was. Everyone noticed it wasn't one of the family's rowboats. When they arrived in Juneau, people noticed it too, but no one claimed it. There wasn't a fisherman who didn't know another fisherman or about another's boat, and no one knew who the boat belonged to.

So Pop brought the boat up on the beach at their home at Marks Trail in Juneau and started to work on it. He checked the boards to see if they were strong enough to hold the new materials he was going to apply, and he found that indeed the boat was strong enough and would hold them.

He began to renew it by stripping the old paint off. Then he caulked up the seams and finally put on some green paint left over from some other boat that he had painted before. He put a pair of oars in that didn't quite match. He tied an old piece of manila rope on the bow that could be used to tie it up.

It was a good-looking boat. It looked just like the flower chalice of a skunk cabbage. And when he tried it, it had balance. It glided across the water very nicely. It was almost as wide as it was long. It was almost round, and because it looked like an eggshell, they called it the "Egg Boat," *Yaakw K'wát'* in Tlingit.

Ḵeixwnéi liked it very much and wanted to try it. She thought the boat was so cute. But when her father told her it was hers, she thought it was the most beautiful boat she had ever seen.

Her own boat! Why, she thought that it was going to be for one of her brothers. She could hardly believe the boat was hers. She was so happy she went around daydreaming about it for the longest time.

Now that she had her own boat, it meant she could go fishing on her own boat alongside her brothers, Auntie, and Grandma all by herself. It also meant she might catch a record-breaking salmon that she would fight for so long that she would get exhausted from just the thought of it.

Or perhaps she and Auntie and Grandma would hit a school of fish like she heard some fishing people talk about. She would fill up her little boat, empty it, then go back out and fill it again.

Or perhaps she would catch her first king salmon, and she wouldn't care what size it was just as long as it was a king.

Her rowboat took her through many adventures during her daydreaming. How exciting the next coho season was going to be! She was so happy.

And now they were actually going to the fishing ground. The boat moved along at a good speed. They all worked on their gear, giving it a last-minute check for weak spots and sections that needed replacing.

Mom steered the boat while Pop checked the tackle he would use on the big boat. She ran the boat a lot, taking over completely, especially when Pop had to do work on deck or when he started catching a lot of salmon. Sometimes she even engineered. There was no pilot-house control, so Pop would ring a bell to signal "slow," "fast," "neutral," "backwater," and so forth.

The boys were playing some kind of game on deck. They said their gear was ready. Keixwnéi's auntie wound her line onto her wooden fishing wheel. Grandma was taking a nap. She had been ready for quite some time. She was always ready for things.

As for Keixwnéi, she had her tackle that her auntie had helped her get together from discarded gear left by various members of the family. She and her auntie had made a line for her while she was still fishing in her auntie's rowboat. Her spinner was the one her father had made for her the previous year from a discarded spoon. It was brass.

Her herring hook, however, was brand new. It was the one her auntie had given her for her own. She was ready to fish, completely outfitted with rubber boots one of her brothers loaned her that were slightly too large.

She was so excited she could hardly eat. The family teased her that she was probably fasting for the record-breaking salmon.

When they finally got near enough to see the fishing ground, there were a lot of powerboats trolling and others were anchored. A lot of the hand-trolling fleet was there too. Some of the hand trollers lived in tents out at Point Adolfus for the duration of the summer. When there were no salmon, the fishing people turned their full attention to smoking halibut they jigged from the bay over past Point Adolfus. Some of the people were relatives of the family.

When they finally reached the fishing ground, everyone was eager to get out and fish. They all took turns jumping into their boats while Pop and the two boys held the rowboats for them while the big boat was still moving along.

Grandma went first, then Auntie Anny, then at last Keixwnéi's turn came. The boys followed in the power skiff that was converted from a tender boat for seining.

They immediately began to troll. Grandma and Auntie Anny went close to the kelp beds along the shoreline. The boys stayed just on the outside of the kelp, while Keixwnéi was all over the place and sometimes dragging the bottom.

She didn't even know where her father, mother, sister, and brothers were. She didn't notice a thing—just that she was going to catch her own salmon. Every time she dragged the bottom she was sure she had a strike.

Evening came and people began to go to their own ports. Grandma and Auntie waited for Keixwnéi for such a long time they thought she wasn't coming in for that night. When they finally got her to come along with them to go back to the *New Anny*, all of a sudden she realized it was near dark and uneasiness came over her. She had completely forgotten all about the kooshdaa kaa stories she had heard, where the Land Otter Man came and took people who were near drowning and kept them captive as one of them. She quickly pulled up her line and came along with Grandma and Auntie Anny.

Everyone had caught salmon except Keixwnéi. It was so disappointing, especially when her brothers teased her about being skunked by saying, "Where's your big salmon, Keixwnéi?" The rest of the family said she would probably catch one the next day and she shouldn't worry. She slept very little that night. Maybe she never ever was going to catch a salmon at all.

The next day the fish buyer who anchored his scow said that there were fish showing up at Home Shore and that he was going over there to buy fish on his tender.

Pop pulled up the anchor to start off for Home Shore. But halfway between Point Adolfus and Home Shore, the boat started to rock back and forth from a storm that had just started to blow. Chatham Strait was stuffed with dark clouds and rain. So they had to make a run for shelter instead of trolling that day—another disappointment for Keixwnéi, especially after standing on deck most of the way straining her eyes to see if anyone was catching any salmon.

They holed up all night. She heard her father getting up from time to time during the night. He never slept much on nights of a storm.

Daybreak was beautiful. It was foggy, but through the fog they could see that the sun was going to be very bright. Where the fog started to drop, the water surface was like a mirror except where the "spine of the tide"—the riptide—made ripples of tiny jumping waves on one side, and the other side had tiny tide navels. Sounds carried far. They could hear gulls cry, and a porpoise breathing somewhere, and splashing from fish jumps. It was going to be gorgeous.

They ate quickly and went off to the fishing ground. Once again they took their turns getting into their boats while the big boat moved along.

This day Keixwnéi stuck really close to her grandma and

auntie. They stayed on the tide spine, circling it as it moved along. She did everything they did. They measured fathoms by the span between their arms from fingertip to fingertip. Keixwnéi also measured her fathoms the same way. She checked her lines for kinks whenever one of them did theirs. She especially stayed close by when Auntie got her first strike of the day. She had hooked a lively one. Keixwnéi circled her and got as close as she dared without the salmon tangling their lines.

Then Grandma got her first salmon of the day.

Keixwnéi had just about given up hope of getting a salmon for that day when she got her first strike. It was so strong that the strap on the main line almost slipped from her hand. She grabbed for it just in time.

Splash! Out of the water jumped the salmon! At the same time—swish!—the salmon took off with her line! The line made a scraping hum on the end of the boat where it was running out.

In the meantime the salmon jumped out into the air and made a gigantic splash. She could hear her grandmother saying, "My little grandchild! It might pull her overboard!" while her auntie said, "Stay calm, stay calm, my little niece. Don't hold on too tight. Let it go when it runs."

Splash! Splash! Splash! Splash! The salmon jumped with her line. It was going wild. It was a while before she could get it near enough to see that it was a coho and a good-sized one too. She would get it close to the boat and then it would take off on the run again. Just when she had it close enough to hit with her gaff-hook club, it would take off again. Several times she hit the water with the club, instead of the fish, because it kept wiggling out of range. Each time the salmon changed its direction the little boat did too, and the salmon pulled the little boat in every direction you could think of. The boat was like a little round dish, and the fish would make it spin.

At long last the salmon tired itself out, and when she pulled it to the boat it just sort of floated on top of the water. She clubbed it one good one. It had no fight left.

She dragged it aboard and everyone around her yelled for joy with her. Grandma and Auntie looked as if they had pulled in the fish. They both said, "Xwei! She's finally got it!" Keixwnéi was sopping wet. Her face was all beaded with water.

It was the only salmon she caught that day, but, by gosh, she brought it in herself! She sold the salmon, and with some of the money she got for it she bought a pie for the family. What a feast that was! Everyone made pleasing comments about her so she could overhear them.

They mainly wished she wouldn't spend all her money on pie and that she was going to start saving her fishing money for important things that a girl should have as she grew older.

It was great to be a troller. That fall was a very memorable one for Keixwnéi. Rain or shine, she tried to rise with Grandma and Auntie each dawn.

One day they all timed it just right for the salmon to feed. Everyone made good that day. There wasn't a fisherman who wasn't happy about his or her catch that day. Keixwnéi also made good. When Auntie and Grandma lined up their salmon on the beach for cleaning, she also had her eight salmon lined up. What a day that was!

When they got to Juneau after the season was over, everyone bought some of the things they'd said they would buy once the season was over. Pop bought some hot dogs for dinner and a watermelon that Grandma called "water berry."

Keixwnéi bought herself a pair of new hip boots. They were dandies! They had red and white stripes all the way around the sole seams. And they also had patches that read "B. F. Goodrich" on each knee. And they fit perfectly if she wore two pairs of socks.

Her mother told her they were a very fine pair and that they would wear for a long time. Now she wouldn't have to borrow boots from her brothers anymore. In fact, they could borrow hers from time to time. And she could use the boots to play make-believe fishing with toy boats she and her brothers made from driftwood bark back home at Marks Trail. And very best of all—she would wear her boots when she went with the family to get fish for dryfish camp on their next trip.

# Magic Gloves

*I*t was June of 1992, and a thousand Tlingit, Haida, and Tsimshian dancers from southeast Alaska were about to converge in Juneau for Celebration '92. Many would be in full regalia, and Grandma Nora was busy designing new things to fill out the dance wardrobes of her grandchildren.

Three Austrian women came as guests to Grandma Nora and Grandpa Dick's house. They had come all the way from the giant city of Vienna and the tiny village of Hörsching in upper Austria, and they could hardly wait for the dancing to begin.

When they arrived, Grandma Nora was working on dance gloves for her grandchildren Teresa, Amelia, Dominic, and Patrick to wear when they performed at the Celebration. The three Austrian women, Käthe, Marianne, and Julia, said, "Let us help you!" because Grandma had too much to do. So Käthe, Marianne, and Julia helped with the gloves.

Grandma Nora showed them what she had in mind, and they sewed one, two, three, four, five pairs. Dominic took the red-trimmed pair. Amelia wanted the pair with aqua trim.

When Dominic tried his on to practice, when Grandma Nora showed him how to dance with them, he stepped into motion as if he had been dancing like that all the ten years of his life. Dominic made his gloves dance. He made the fringes fly, he made the fingers wiggle, he made the hands quiver and tremble like a sockeye salmon swimming up a shallow summer stream. The gloves were magic, and he made them come alive. As he danced with his new gloves, their three Austrian creators took photographs and movies, and immortalized the moment.

Nora's grandson Dominic dancing in *The Magic Gloves*. (Photograph by Käthe Recheis)

Nora's nieces—Marcie, Rachel, and Dawn Joel—performing a Raven dance.

Pat Helle and her husband, Bob, and their two children, Katrina and Jon, were also staying at Grandma Nora's house. They had come from Vancouver, Washington, to join the Celebration. When Pat saw that Grandma Nora still had felt dancing tunics to make for Dominic and Patrick, she volunteered to help. That day they sewed for about five hours. They made two cute tunics with fringe on the bottom, to accompany the magic gloves. The fringe on the tunics also danced along with the gloves.

Several years before, Grandpa Dick had boiled the hooves from all the deer that he and Uncle Dewey and Uncle Sy and the other hunters in the family had taken. He had cleaned them and drilled a hole in each one. Now Auntie Carm and Auntie Leonora tied each hoof to a leather string and dangled sets of them together from a leather tie-string so that they and Amelia and Dominic and Patrick and whoever wanted them could wear the hoofs around their legs, make noise when they danced, and turn their bodies into rattles.

Two months before the Celebration, Grandpa Dick had visited Siberia and had spent some time with Khanty reindeer herders tenting in their remote winter camps. He brought back a beaded belt for whichever granddaughter it would fit. It was made by a Khanty reindeer herding girl named Anna, who gave the belt to Grandpa Dick on his birthday for one of the girls in his family to wear. The belt fit Amelia, and she wore it to enhance her magic gloves while she drummed.

All of these magic gifts of handicraft and love made the best gear for Tlingit dancing in Celebration '92. The night the children performed on center stage, the hands with which Amelia took up her drum and drumstick were gloved with aqua trim—another magic pair, coming alive as she turned her drumbeat into the heartbeat of the group, and the feet of the family dancers moved in time with friends and relatives from around the world.

# Chemawa Cemetery
## Buried in Alien Land

*T*he graveyard is small. Across the railroad tracks from Chemawa Indian School, it seems tiny compared to the land around it, and to the old red-brick school. But when you start looking at the graves of kids who never made it back home, it seems huge.

As we sang the Russian Orthodox Panikhida (the requiem service for the dead), I remembered from way back in another container of my memory how my father told me about the experiences of Alaska Native students attending the Indian school.

He said the most terrible was when they remembered their Indian foods back at home as they passed from bunk to bunk raw potatoes they swiped to eat after lights-out. Someone would make the sounds of salmon boiling with seal oil and water cooking on a beach or elsewhere out of doors. They could almost taste the broth.

Even wearing the clothing issued to the students was difficult. In fear the students might steal something or put their hands in their pockets, they were given pants without pockets. Most of our people had wider feet than Caucasians from running without footwear. If anything was worn, it was rubber boots. But they issued narrow shoes to kids whose feet were used to freedom. My father's feet were squeezed out of shape and distorted from wearing their shoes. As he got older, his feet were in pain at all times for the rest of his life.

He was very sad when he told me about one of the boys from his hometown, and of how he was whipped in sewer and toilet water and how the schoolteachers or guards dunked his head under and held it there for a few moments. My father was sure the student nearly drowned in the liquid. As the student grew older, his voice became weaker.

My father remembered how lonely he, too, felt when the youngest students cried for home and their parents and were punished and sent to bed without food.

He told me how he and his brother Peter and another Tlingit boy ran away from the school by taking a rowboat and floating down a river; how as they were floating at night they heard a thunder just before seeing the falls they were about to go over. They instantly tried to row upriver against the flow or even row to the bank. The boy going along with them yelled at them to make for a log sticking out over the river from the bank. When they came close enough, the boy buried the hatchet they had brought along in the log, and the three boys managed to pull themselves ashore.

They all made it to the Oregon coast and met with Indians there, who gave them food and shelter. I think maybe they were Siletz, but my father wasn't sure. By coincidence, I was invited there a few years ago and hosted by these people, who I like to think were the folks who saved my father. They stayed only until their parents could send them money to come home.

I thought of these things as we looked over the graves of those who never made it home, finding students from many places in Alaska, the early victims of a new educational system for Alaska Native people and other Native Americans. My uncle Peter spent the rest of his life in Alaska and passed away in the late 1920s. In the 1970s my father, my mother, my three brothers, and my sister were hired in various capacities to teach in the Juneau School District Indian studies program, so my father at least lived to see a change in Indian education. He passed away in August 1981.

In the 1970s, my father visited the East Coast with our dance group. He looked at Plymouth Rock without saying much. "This the Atlantic Ocean?" he asked. A North Pacific fisherman all his life, he gazed with appreciation, understanding, and satisfaction at the North Atlantic. And at Salem, Massachusetts, he quipped, "I've already seen Salem, Oregon."

# Life Woven with Song
## An Autobiographical Essay

### FIRST MEMORIES OF ART

*I* know it was a wonderful day, sunny, by looking at the green, translucent leaves that curtained the space between a spruce bough and the surface of the earth. The earth I could smell was an open one. I could see silhouettes walking and bending over at intervals. I felt I knew them. I could see bundles of turf rolled up like bales of cotton, at least three of them. One slightly to my left, another at an angle to the right of me, and I could see only a crescent section of the last one, with shade-filtered light. I could make out the brown earth that I smelled with roots that looked like a giant drawing of a being with its veins exposed. The two or three people who were bending and walking at intervals were cutting and pulling the veins. The people were my grandmother, my aunt (my father's older sister), and a teenage girl named Shaa X̱aatk'í. When they were done, they unrolled the bales of turf to cover the bed of roots again.

At a later time in my life this haunting image kept coming back to me. I asked my mother if she remembered such an incident in my early life. After thinking about it, she told me I went with my grandmother to pick spruce roots near Elfin Cove. Grandma Eliza and Auntie Anny, with Alice, were picking spruce roots to weave into spruce root baskets. This is the earliest I remember going for natural materials to be made into art.

Another time, it was midday. My grandmother was sitting in a nest of timothy grass near a playhouse. She looked like a little girl getting ready to go into the playhouse. She was so tiny she'd fit in nicely. She seemed to have the grass tangling around her fingers and hands. I could smell the strong, fresh grass. I could also hear the snapping as she broke the stalks of grass against her thumbnail. Beside her was a pile of grass broken at the joints. She kept on breaking these grasses at their joints. In the next image I remember the grass in a pan with water. They looked like logs lashed together by loggers in a bay. The house was filled with the aroma. In my next memory I see the grass lashed together, hanging up to dry on nails on a wall. Next to them were coiled in figure eights the spruce roots for baskets.

The winter was cold. We were living somewhere in a tent. I could hear my grandmother's squeaky thumb and index finger moving along a wet weft of a spruce root basket. Grandma Eliza always moved slowly in whatever she did, but she was steady. Her baskets were always rising in beauty. She put the old, geometric designs on her baskets. Auntie Anny wove fast, and her work always looked the beautiful color of cockle flesh. She wove bluebirds, butterflies, and roses into her rattletop baskets. When both Grandma and Auntie wove they both made squeaky sounds together. Next to them were coils of split spruce roots and split timothy grass to run around the baskets, row upon row, in their favorite designs.

Auntie Jennie was a bead worker and skin sewer. She was very good at keeping children quiet, too. Early in my life she made dolls for me that we kept in a raisin box. The dolls were made from old cloths that had drops of seal oil on them. They smelled like seal oil and raisins when we played with them. We gave them names and carried on a dialogue as the dolls' voices. They came to life as our relatives. I have many fond memories of Auntie Jennie such as these from various periods of my life. From time to time, they find their way into poems, such as "My Auntie Jennie's Bed."

Once when Auntie Jennie was beading moccasin tops, she made me string red and white beads onto a thread. She drew a strawberry on a tiny moccasin top with a pencil. Then she showed me how to bead a strawberry: First outline them, then fill in with beads. They looked wonderful, even with all the knots and tangles of threads on both sides of the top. She said, "Even when strawberries are ripe they're never the same size or look the same." She cleaned it up and made moccasins with it. In this way they became real.

My father logged yellow cedar from many areas. He looked for trees that had a nice grain. He was a grand carver. He carved for four shops and the Alaska Native Arts Co-op, ANAC Cache. He made miniature totems and life-sized masks. In the boat or house or tent, every corner would have the scent of yellow cedar. He carved a lot, so all of us children learned to steer clear of his work area, especially where he kept his razor-sharp knives and the liquid paint he used on his totems and masks. When he began painting, his totems took on a new look. His masks took on a very mythic personality—the Kooshdaa ḵaa (Land Otter Man), Frog Man, fish mask, Blackskin, and Lady, all representing stories I heard falling asleep.

During the day, focus was on the work to keep alive and warm. After the evening meal, all of the men who were along on hunting or trapping participated in storytelling. This is when I would be pulled in and woven along into the stories. I imagined every incident or tragic ending as real. If we listened carefully, we kids could practice telling the stories to each other later. I usually fell asleep listening to the storytelling.

When I went to sleep, Grandma Eliza and Auntie Anny would be weaving their baskets; when I would awaken, they were still weaving. I sometimes thought they never slept and wove all night. Auntie Jennie was one who sewed. She never stopped her sewing, either; while she sewed she whistled through her teeth. She never seemed to tire.

At times I'd watch my father line up his miniature totems, all painted first with black lines, then the blue lines, then red lines, then some brown or some yellow. Then he would pack them in a box with newspaper or magazine pages to keep the paint that hadn't dried yet from touching the other totems. If we were in town, he took the totems to a merchant who bought them and sold them to tourists. When my father was in a hurry, my mother helped him paint the totems. They laughed at how their work appeared to them.

After he sold them, he would bring down to the boat or the house at Marks Trail groceries and a box of day-old pastries for treats, and for adults to eat with tea or coffee. My father loved wine. He sometimes made enough money to buy this too, which sometimes ran away with him. Other than this, he was a wonderful father.

My father was the youngest of four brothers. Every one of them was a carver and boat builder who came from a long line of artists and boat builders in Hoonah. During the winter, on bad days when they couldn't go out to hunt or trap, the men would carve something, after taking care of the camp's shelters and wood supply. The women took care of food and clothing. At times they made warm, thick mittens and insulators to wear inside shoe packs for when the men hunted in freezing weather. They mended shirts, coats, sweaters, and pants for both men and children in the evenings.

## GAMES AND CHORES

On bad-weather days we would stay inside the tent that the wind would puff up and deflate. I still love to listen to the wind rustling through the trees around us. Because our indoor living space was so crowded, we enjoyed outdoor activities. If we kids dressed warm, we got to play out in the wind. At such times we created many ways in which to play. One of them was playing with the wind. We would see how much we'd have to push if we ran against it. We'd talk to each other, but our voices were blown off with the wind. We let it carry us along, then we'd turn and run against it.

On nice days we played with boats we made from driftwood. These are called kooxwás' in Tlingit. We waited until the tide was over the gravel above the seaweeded beach. We played with bubbles as the tide came in. I know some children today who would love playing on the beaches we played on with our driftwood boats. We had so much fun. We would tie a yard-long string to the bow of the boat, then tie the other end to a stick about a yard or more long. Then we dragged the boats by the end of the sticks, taking them into coves. We acted the roles of the boat captains, deckhands, and cooks. The captain would say to the cook, "Got some coffee down there?" Cook always answered, "There's a little left. I'll make some more. Do you want the last of it?" Captain answered, "Yes!"

At times our play crew unloaded salmon to a fish buyer. The fish buyer would ask the captain, "How's fishing today, Alex?" He'd answer, "Not bad." All this dialogue went on in Tlingit. When there was a monolingual English-speaking captain, we only imitated the language by what it sounded like to us because none of us could speak English. We spoke only in Tlingit.

During severe cold spells we played two-person string games called tleilk'óo in Tlingit. We passed the forms back and forth. Our favorite Tlingit game was the one called K'ich'óo. We played it similar to a dice game. This game was taught to us by our uncle John. He carved an object that looked like a tiny chair, one and a quarter inch square. We would throw this on a flat surface and call out by which way it fell, sidewise with the back down or in a sitting position. You'd win if the chair landed in a sitting position. We played this while the wind whipped everything around us.

We also played a wind and whistle game called xoon kayénaa, "Stringer of the North Wind." The wind and whistle toy was made like a big button with two holes and a strong string drawn through the two holes, then tied at the end. To play you twisted away or toward you the two-hole object while holding by the string on each end. When the strings on each end start to twist up, you start pulling on each end at once and relaxing after every pull. Each time you pulled on the string, the object made a wuffing sound from the wind it created. We took turns passing the object from one child to the next while it was still turning, to see how long we could keep it going. We were not allowed to play this one just any time in the winter, but only when it was already too wet and rainy. The belief was the toy would be an instrument to start the north wind, so we didn't play with it too much. We played this game when we wanted a cold spell, usually toward the afternoon or evening, after our chores were done.

Our chores were to roll up our beds when we got up in the morning. On good days we'd shake out our bedding outside and air them out. After breakfast we gathered driftwood that was twisted along the beach by ocean waves for the tank stoves my father and uncles made for us to cook on and to keep the tents warm. On wash day we carried water for the wash, and everyone washed their clothes and bedding, and dried them in the sun and wind. On cold days the wash froze.

During the summer on nice, sunny days my father took us on the home fishing boat to anchor off a stream where we could wash all our soiled clothes. We would bring along bar soap, washboards, and washtubs. We all washed and dried our clothes on hot rocks; the heavy clothing, like jeans, we hung on low-hanging tree boughs. Because it was sometimes so hot, we didn't have to warm the water over a fire, but if we left it in a washtub it warmed enough to wash in, so we filled every container first. Mom washed the baby's clothing and hers and Father's. All the kids who were able washed their own clothes and the little ones helped by washing their own socks. In some cases the older ones helped them to wash them over again. When all the wash was done, we would wring our clothes out into a giant quilt, and the trees seemed like they were hung with flags.

The subsistence lifestyle that our extended family followed required us to be self-sufficient. My father learned to do makeshift welding if something important broke when we were living in remote camps. Folk medicine was also important and kept us alive. Some of these memories took shape in the poem "Grandmother Eliza."

## BOAT BUILDING

When my uncles and my father built their boats, they bent and steamed the prow, keel, and rib planks. Of course, this method wasn't new to them. Before any English or Russian sailor appeared on the horizon, our people made great canoes, some seagoing and others for rivers, light enough to portage over glaciers and then on the return to come out under glaciers. They were made from cedar logs, which were then steamed open with hot rocks and water.

Bending by steam was nothing new to them. My father had a hot-water tank he put over a fire with water inside. First he steamed the ribs, then he steamed the planks to curve and fit to the ribs of the boat. I often think now about the way they did this. I never questioned the way they did this or even thought about it. It was natural for them to build their boats in this way. I never thought my father did high-tech boat building with innovations of his own. My father built rowboats for Grandma and Auntie. He built a boat for himself and my mother when they got married. He—with his brothers, his older son, Alex, and his nephews, David Williams, Willie Williams, and Horace Marks—rebuilt many boats. He rebuilt mine—a dinghy about eight feet long that we called the "Egg Boat" and that inspired a short story many years later. I fished many summers. Each time they refinished an old boat, it took on a new look and became more handsome, as all the grime fell from its face.

Getting ready for salmon seining was very complicated. Before fishing, my father and brothers began mending their seine net. A seine is a kind of drawstring net used to catch salmon from large fishing boats called seine boats. It is called a purse seine because the net is drawn together at the bottom like a purse. My childhood memories are of the men doing this by hand and coming in from work with their hands dried, cracked, and bent into a gripping shape. After World War II a mechanized block-and-tackle technology was introduced called a power block, which made pulling the seine easier.

The smell of the web was very strong. Nowadays, from time to time, I still smell it in my mind, with the scent of tar and bluestone, which was some kind of a chemical bath mixture that my father dipped his net in to keep the jellyfish away. They mended their webs by using a shuttle with web-mending line in it. They measured each mesh from cross corner to cross corner, four and one-quarter inches for each mesh, called waak̲ (eye) in Tlingit.

Purse seiners hauling in their net.

In early spring my father cleaned the bottom of our boat. This involved scrubbing off all the barnacles that grew on the hull. After the scrubbing and cleaning, Pop and his crew painted the bottom with copper paint up to the waterline. Occasionally we helped with painting. If Pop didn't let us, it was because we didn't do a good job.

Our extended family used to fish off of several boats. For safety, we usually traveled together in a small fleet of two, three, or four boats. The crew consisted of my uncles, my father's sister's sons, and my brothers. Some of my childhood memories of the boat are worked into poems, such as "A Poem for Jim Nagataak'w."

## MUSIC AND SONG

When Saturday came around and seine boats appeared around the point at the Icy Strait cannery, after unloading and cleaning the boat and sitting down, Pop and his nephews and sons would bring out their guitars on the deck of the *New Anny,* tied to a float. ("Floats" are the floating sections of the dock to which the boats tie up. They rise and fall with the tide. The main pier or dock is fixed on pilings. A ramp called a gangway or gangplank connects the pier and the float.) Their music carried on the water, amplified by the calm, summer-evening sea. Many young fishermen still remember this even today. I asked my mother where they learned to play. She said, "Your father and his brother took lessons from a Hawaiian who lived in Juneau. He also taught your dad and his brother to dance Hawaiian hula." My father taught his clan sisters so they could dance at his brother's memorial, because my uncle loved Hawaiian music and dance so much.

The family was very musical. All my aunts and uncles sang in the Russian Orthodox church. They were also ceremonial singers for potlatches, called in Tlingit K̲oo.éex'. My oldest uncle composed songs in Tlingit. He composed them for his brother's children. We still sing them today.

As I look back on my youth and childhood, I realize how much songs and music formed a good part of our lives. My extended family and my father and aunts all composed Tlingit songs. The most important of them was Shkík, my Aunt Mary's mother, and the grandmother of my cousin Elizabeth Govina. Shkík was a shaman (íx̲t' in Tlingit). She had many spirit helpers and songs. Her spirit helpers are still singing today, through the visual art pieces depicting those spirits that my father carved as ceremonial commissions. These pieces are used in ceremonials for the removal of grief. Mrs. Lindoff, who was Aunt Mary's aunt, also composed many songs, as did her brother, Johnny C. Johnson. One of the most popular songs is about Tlingit elder Amy Marvin, and it is still sung today by the Hoonah Mount Fairweather Dancers.

On my father's side, Uncle Jim Marks composed songs about the women he loved. His brother John also composed songs. My father's clan sister by the name of L̲x̲oo k̲ composed many songs that are still sung in Hoonah. My paternal grandfather, Jakwteen, came from a river where you could hear the people singing above the noise of the river. He composed, as did his relatives from Chilkat. His cousin John Marks and Jack David, my Auntie Jennie's brother, were song leaders. A relative named K'eedzaa composed one of the favorite songs performed by our family dance group today. One of my mother's relatives, K'uxaach, builder of the Canoe Prow House along the Alsek River, also composed many songs, but we have been able to save only two of them.

Lullabies were an early part of our lives as children. When we were old enough to stand, my grandfather would sing lullabies to us and we would dance to them. My cousin Betty, who was the oldest of the grandchildren, danced every time our grandfather started to sing. One time he told her, "A kínt iyahán, Chxánk'," literally "You're not standing close enough," but a euphemism hinting that one needs to improve one's dancing. Little Betty took him literally and thought she should move out a little until she had moved so close to the stove that she was nearly burning! One of my uncles composed lullabies for the girls in the family and sang lullabies for the boys. He had nicknames by which he called all the boys.

As we grew older, work songs became part of our lives. Whether we were cutting up salmon or picking berries, you could hear my aunts and grandmother singing. Today, I sing these lullabies and songs for my grandchildren and great-grandchild. Here's one of my favorites, which I translated into English. The words work out fairly well to the Tlingit melody and drumbeat.

Let's go up the hill,
little girls.
I thought I saw
elderberry blossoms there.
It was her gray hair
that I saw,
that I saw
there.

This is the art I grew up with. My whole family is artistic. My brothers are still carvers, and my sister Florence and my mother are still artists in beadwork. My mother had a one-person show of her art at the Alaska State Museum in March 1988 entitled "Wax, Facets and Felt: Beadwork by Emma Marks." My cousin Betty, Uncle John's daughter, has a Tlingit art shop on the dock in Juneau where tourists disembark.

The only artist in the family who went "worldwide" was my uncle David Williams. He was my father's nephew, his sister's son, and in English would be considered a "cousin" but in Tlingit a paternal uncle, because he is not of my clan. He concentrated on his art in two different ways. One was to make traditional art for the village of Hoonah, where many of his original pieces still remain and are still in ceremonial use. The other was to make art for art's sake, beyond the context of his community, the way many Western artists do. The numerous pieces he created this way now reside mostly in private ownership. He traveled widely, including to England, where he demonstrated his carving for royalty and had an audience with the queen.


SCHOOL AND CHURCH

Our family has lived for five (now starting six) generations on a small piece of land on Douglas Island, across the Gastineau Channel from Juneau. There was no road when I was a child, so we had to walk along the beach for about half an hour to meet the school bus. Taxis would also drop us off at that point. Before the Juneau–Douglas bridge was finished in the mid-1930s, the family would row across the channel to shop, go to movies, or go to church. The family believed in a higher power, and my uncle set aside time for prayer wherever we were. On Sunday, we all rowed across for services at St. Nicholas Russian Orthodox Church. Whenever we were in Hoonah, we were also active in church activities, especially meetings and choir practice. Often these were held in the clan houses. When we went to church school, I tried to learn to read Russian prayers. As I look back on things, I guess I had the desire to go to school all along.

But going to school wasn't easy. During my childhood, truant officers often detained families such as ours, forcing them to settle in towns. This made it impossible to pursue the traditional seasonal subsistence economy, so elders were suspicious of school authorities. When we stopped in Hoonah or Juneau on the boat, my father and the rest of the family hid the children from the school authorities. My brothers, sisters, and I were so restless we were like bees in a beehive, ready to drone out of the boat the minute we were allowed to go outside.

At one point while we older children were going to school in Hoonah, we took our little brother Raymond along. We never heard the end of that all during our growing up! Whenever we got to Juneau, the family would have liked my father to stay for a little while longer and settle down for the rest of the winter. Eventually, we children ended up in school full time. For me, at the age of eight, it was my first exposure to English, having grown up until that time in a culturally conservative, monolingual Tlingit-speaking environment. I have mixed memories of school. The first memories are of being rapped across the knuckles with a ruler for speaking Tlingit, and of always being blamed and punished for reasons I didn't understand, for which I didn't know enough English to explain or defend myself. I could defend myself pretty well with my fists on the playground, though. I used to beat up boys for hitting me with snowballs and for teasing me. I even chased them into the boys' bathroom to beat them up! Usually they became my friends after I beat them up.

When I turned sixteen, I was all set to go to school at Sheldon Jackson School in Sitka. I had money that I made from my first job in one of the canneries that I was to work at throughout my life as a mother and housewife (more about this below). But when my grandmother got wind of my plans, her only comment was, "She might as well take my head with her!" And that was the end of my education for many years.

Our first to graduate from high school was Horace Marks, my cousin; then there was Ron Williams, another cousin; and my brother, Alex Marks. There were many others who followed. Some are kids from the *New Anny,* others from my uncle's boat, the *Urania.*

I would like to note here that Horace went on from high school to become the Alaska Native Brotherhood Grand Camp secretary in the late 1930s and early 1940s. He was also involved with the forming of Indian Reorganization Act councils. His older brother, Austin Hammond, gave us wisdom to continue into the twenty-first century. He went on to be the leader of Raven House and an officer in the Salvation Army. When some religions asked how he could be a leader of Raven House and a leader in the Salvation Army, he responded, "God made us to be Tlingit and to continue our culture." He didn't see the need to abandon our culture. Several years ago he set up a culture camp, Lkoot Kwáan (People of Chilkoot), where our youths can learn about being good human beings. He left to us of the Lukaax.ádi clan a trust of Raven House for us to continue to practice our culture. To help our education in Tlingit culture, language, literature, and the use of land, Austin and his brother Horace worked with a filmmaker to document his argument for Lukaax.ádi land in Chilkoot. The state had withdrawn many Lukaax.ádi sites, mostly historical, around Haines. The film is now available in home-video format, and a more recent video documents his life (*Haa Shagóon* and *Daanawáak, for the Children,* respectively, both available from Sealaska Heritage Foundation in Juneau).

With the help of my father's third-grade education from Chemawa Indian School, and with his own Tlingit knowledge of land ownership, my grandfather, Jim Nagatáak'w, applied for ownership of the land my family had settled on in Juneau and has been living on and using now for six generations. He and my father camped at the door of the Bureau of Land Management office until the bureaucrats tired of them and started proceedings for them to gain title to the land now called Marks Trail (named after the logging trail blazed by my grandfather). They applied for land in 1916 and received the deed for it in 1921. My father and grandfather stood at the government door until they softened the path to their land. Most of my grandfather's original land was lost to the miners, but what remains is one of the few parcels of land still in Tlingit possession.

Up until the 1960s Pop and Mom raised us on Native foods. They supplemented them with Western foods bought with totem pole, seining, beadwork, and basketry money. Seasonal cannery work was also a major source of cash income for the women, and most of us worked in canneries for many years. I guess we had fun. But, in retrospect, it is sobering to be more conceptually aware of the discrimination we all experienced, especially segregated housing. The white men's bunkhouse had showers and toilets, whereas the Indian families lived in cabins with no toilets or running water. But this experience, like others, gave rise to poetry, such as "Salmon Egg Puller," with its opening line "You learn to dance with machines."

## TLINGIT RENAISSANCE

In 1968 my uncle Jim Marks passed away, leaving Auntie Jennie a widow. She set aside this retirement stage of her life to teach us Tlingit dancing, and we formed the Marks Trail Dancers in 1968. She taught us our Lukaax̱.ádi clan songs and we danced to them. We became a popular group. As far as I know, we were the first such organized dance group, with membership from different clans, that traveled and performed on invitation. If not the first, we were certainly one of the first. Up to that time, songs and dances were mostly performed in ceremonial contexts only and by members of a single clan, or at non-Tlingit civic events such as the dedication of libraries and such. Now, twenty-five years later, more than a thousand dancers gather every other year in Juneau for a Tlingit folk festival called Celebration.

I often think back to our first public performance, at an annual Tlingit and Haida convention. We had only one song in our repertoire, which we called in English "Go for Broke." Composed by a clansman named K̲'astook̲ Eesh (who lived before the arrival of English family names), the song describes the disruption and dys-

Nora's brother John and Auntie Jennie Marks singing.

function of cultural contact and changing times, and urges people to band together in love and mutual support.

Pop got excited and made me a rattle. Mom was also excited and made us dance jewelry and tunics. I made button robes for friends and fund-raisers. Our brother John and Mom made ear yarns for dancing our special dances. My father and mother, with the help of my brother, made a set of Raven wings and headdress in which my daughter Le performed the Raven dance. Mom made me a dance tunic that I still wear. My father later made me a headdress called Geesán Shakee.át and sent it to me for Christmas. I unveiled it at Auntie Jennie's memorial.

I taught Tlingit in the Juneau high school for a semester in the early 1970s, but I was not rehired. The official district plan was, because of the demands of accreditation, to replace me with a Tlingit teacher with certification. Now, almost a quarter of a century later, they still have not located a certified Tlingit instructor, nor have they found any other way to teach the Tlingit language on a regular basis.

By this time we were splitting off into educational institutions. My daughter Le went off to Harvard. After my children were out of school, I completed my GED and went off to college at Alaska Methodist University in Anchorage, where I received formal training in linguistics and folklore. I graduated in 1976 with a B.A. in anthropology with a concentration in Tlingit literature. At the university I began the literary work that is now finding its way into publication some twenty years later.

While I was at the university I read *Beowulf* and *Njal's Saga*. They seemed so Tlingit to me in their concern with funerals and family trees. I read Homer, Ferlinghetti, e. e. cummings, Basho, John Haines, Gary Snyder, Dennis Tedlock, and Han Shan. They became some of my teachers. I transcribed and translated Jessie Dalton and the rest of the oratory delivered at my uncle Jim Marks's memorial as a directed study with R. L. Dauenhauer, who would later become my husband. I realized later that these Tlingit orators had become my instructors in Tlingit literature.

As younger Native American writers began to appear in print, I became excited and inspired initially by their work and subsequently by meeting in person Simon Ortiz, James Welch, Joy Harjo, Luci Tapahonso, and others. (I still get excited by the work of new generations of Native American writers.) I also began to discover the work of earlier Native writers such as D'Arcy McNickle.

Following my first year at the university, I was hired by Dr. Michael Krauss of the University of Alaska–Fairbanks to do field work with Tlingit elders in southeast Alaska as a project of the Alaska Native Language Center (ANLC). These elders also became my instructors as I worked with them. Some of them gave me advice when I worked with them; others told me off and declined to have their traditions documented. Working with the ANLC helped me to be in the right place at the right time and to tape-record many elders who have since passed on. We are still working with this backlog. This work gives rise to mixed emotions. On the one hand, it gives me great delight to restore and polish these priceless gems of Tlingit oral literature, composed by the great masters of the tradition. On the other hand, it can be stressful always to be dealing with death, dying, and grief.

## TLINGIT LANGUAGE AND
## ORAL LITERATURE RESEARCH

Because the last quarter century of my life has been devoted in large part to documenting Tlingit language and oral literature, a few words are in order here about bilingual education in Alaska and about events in recent Alaska Native cultural history that are directly related to my current work. (For a more detailed treatment of how schooling, land withdrawals, and other sociopolitical issues have impacted contemporary Tlingit culture, see the book by Nora Marks Dauenhauer and Richard Dauenhauer, *Haa Kusteeyí, Our Culture: Tlingit Life Stories*. During the Russian period in Alaskan history, bilingual schooling was the norm, with instruction provided in Russian and in various Native languages. Russian was required as the common language of the empire, but no effort was made to eliminate Alaska Native languages and replace them with Russian. Russia sold Alaska to the United States in 1867, and with the American period the national policy of instruction only in English was rigorously enforced, with the specific exclusion and prohibition of Native languages, and physical punishment for speaking them. The expressed intent was to eradicate Native languages and cultures and replace them with English. These policies caused irreparable damage to Alaska Native language and culture, and to the individual sense of personhood and self-esteem. As late as 1912, the U.S. government closed by force some of the remaining Orthodox parochial schools that still offered Native languages as a subject of study and used them as a medium of instruction. The English-only policies continued well into the 1960s, and their cumulative emotional impact remains a powerful barrier to the survival of Alaska Native languages today.

Gradually, beginning with the late 1960s and especially in the

1970s, some people began to try to turn this around. For most Alaska Native languages—including Tlingit—it was probably too late. But a few of my generation began to teach our languages and to work with our elders to document their knowledge through tape recording, transcribing, and translating. Writing things down in the Native languages was a new concept, as popular literacy had not been encouraged for most languages for over a hundred years. I worked with Constance Naish and Gillian Story of the Summer Institute of Linguistics/Wycliffe Bible Translators, and with Michael Krauss, to learn the new, popular orthography.

In the 1970s bilingual education was a highly emotional and hotly debated topic locally and nationally, and it remains so. Many school administrators resisted it, and many Native parents were confused by efforts to have the school recognize and teach the very languages that had literally been beaten out of them during their school years. In 1972, Alaska passed bilingual legislation that allowed and even encouraged bilingual programs but still left high-intensity English-as-a-second-language programs as an option. Looking back from three decades later, we see that most districts, on the model of mainstreaming immigrants such as Filipinos and Vietnamese, applied these options to Natives as well. But the main difference is that Native American people were invaded. Unlike German, Spanish, and other immigrant languages in the United States, we have no other homeland; if our languages die out here, they will be gone forever.

After finishing my B.A. degree, I continued to work on Tlingit with my husband. Most of this work was an overload, late into the night, in addition to our regular jobs. In 1983, we decided to move to Juneau to be closer to our family, and to devote ourselves more fully to Tlingit. My husband resigned his university position in Anchorage.

We bought land uphill from my mother's beach property on Douglas Island, across from Juneau. The land we bought was originally part of my grandfather's land that was taken during the gold rush and eventually subdivided by the descendants of the original miners. At that time, Natives were not able to file claims, but miners could claim Native land right up to the houses the Natives occupied. We bought it back, built our house, and built a new smokehouse on the beach.

After we moved to Juneau, jobs opened up for us at the Sealaska Heritage Foundation (SHF), an Alaska Native nonprofit organization, where I was principal researcher in language and cultural studies from 1983 to 1997, when the board decided to "downsize" and "outsource" our program. I worked primarily with transcribing, translating, and publishing Tlingit oral literature. Founded in 1980, SHF has the mandate to work with the Native languages and cultures of southeast Alaska: Tlingit, Haida, and Tsimshian. *Sealaska* is an acronym for "Southeast Alaska." The Heritage Foundation is a nonprofit affiliate of the Sealaska Corporation, one of the thirteen regional corporations formed as part of the Alaska Native Claims Settlement Act (ANCSA) of 1971. All of the above requires some additional background.


## A BIT MORE BACKGROUND

Within two years after Alaska was sold by Russia to the United States in 1867, the Tlingit leaders lodged a formal protest, claiming that they and other Native people were the legal owners of the land and had not been consulted or considered in the land deal, much less paid for the land taken from them. American Indian tribes are specifically mentioned in the U.S. Constitution, and it is the task of the United States Congress to deal with Indians on the same basis as with other sovereign nations.

U.S. Indian policy has evolved over the two centuries of our national history, moving from eradication (genocide) to removal (to reservations) to assimilation to termination. As Thomas Berger points out in *A Long and Terrible Shadow: White Values, Native Rights in the Americas, 1492–1992*, the law has almost always been on the side of the Indians, but since the days of Andrew Jackson the political realities of frontier life and westward expansion have not favored the Indians. As President Jackson pointed out, he had an army and the Supreme Court did not.

Two related issues are involved: Native land and Native identity. From the Native point of view, a number of laws have worked against both. For example, the Dawes Act of 1887 was designed to break cooperative ownership of reservation land: Land was allotted to individual owners, and tribal relations were broken. Once individualized, land can be bought by non-Natives or taken by local governments for back taxes, etc. The Dawes Act and similar acts are like a tree uprooted and blown over in the wind, each sprout or root attempting to create a new role for the Indian in American society. The various laws sought to assimilate Indian people by making them into farmers, factory workers, TV repairmen, beauticians, and so on. The programs often involved relocation. The latest phase has been to create corporate businesspeople.

In Alaska, there are several landmarks leading us to the present day. In 1902, the first forest reserve was established, and in 1907 this was transformed into the Tongass National Forest. It included all land not previously homesteaded or claimed by miners or canneries. Because of canneries, the Tlingit had lost legal access to streams and waterways, and now the land base was confiscated as well. In 1912, the Alaska Native Brotherhood (ANB) was founded. It is the oldest Native American organization of its kind still in existence. At their 1929 convention, its members resolved to sue the U.S. government for land taken without payment. The case moved slowly from one piece of enabling legislation to another through the 1930s, '40s, '50s, and '60s, involving the creation of the Central Council of Tlingit and Haida Indian Tribes of Alaska, and the Alaska Federation of Natives. It came to a head through a trespass suit against the oil companies in the late 1960s, blocking development of Alaska North Slope oil. Now, forty years after the ANB resolution, and over a hundred years since the purchase of Alaska, the government had to resolve the question of Native ownership of Alaska land.

The solution came in 1971 in the form of ANCSA. This is a complex act, and it is still being implemented and amended. Essentially, it recognizes aboriginal ownership and provides for a cash settlement and land transfer, but with neither cash nor land to be given directly to individuals. Instead, profit-making corporations were created for twelve regions of Alaska, with a thirteenth corporation for Alaska Natives living outside of Alaska. As noted above, Sealaska is the corporation for southeast Alaska. Investments and land use are managed and dividends are distributed by the corporations. All living qualified Alaska Natives born before December 18, 1971, are counted as shareholders.

One unresolved aspect of ANCSA is the enrollment of, and issuing of new stock to, those born after 1971. ANCSA specifically extinguishes all aboriginal claims, and aboriginal ethnicity is replaced by the concept of the shareholder, yet we now have two generations of disenfranchised Natives, among them most of my grandchildren and my first great-grandchild.


CONCLUSION

My life now is in many respects the opposite of my childhood. Then, we lived much of the year on our boat and in hunting, fishing, and trapping camps in "the bush." We came to town only for provisions. Now it's a treat to go out on a boat.

Coming to town in my childhood put us into first contact with whites. With this contact came our first experience with racism. From the first time I saw white hate I experienced racism as a white-hot whip that can bring you to your knees with one strike. As a child, the stares of children were so hot and cruel that I cowered and wanted to hide and never come out again. I tried to shield my little brothers I was babysitting with my arms. I had nowhere to run with them. Once, the boat we were on had dried up on the tidal flats, and it was too high for me to take my brothers down from the deck. So we stood and took the rain of spears from their eyes until they left us alone because the tide was coming in and they couldn't taunt us anymore. Even now, after many decades,

White Raven beadwork by Nora's mother, Emma Marks. (Photograph by Suzi Jones)

I'm still stinging from their white whip. These patterns still exist; they are alive and well today, and it hurts to see my grandchildren experience it. This was a negative aspect of growing up, and I try to be assertive today to help defend our youngest generations from the same patterns of abuse.

On the positive side, all through my childhood I was surrounded by artists at work. It was a necessity to bring groceries into the house. I'm sure my father was influenced by his mother's brothers and uncles. He didn't try to make a first-rate piece of art for tourist sale. The market didn't give him the price he wanted for it. Only after the 1944 Hoonah fire was he commissioned with his brother Jim for first-rate pieces when he carved ceremonial art such as the Mount Fairweather Hat and Mountain Tribe's Dog Hat. He put his heart and true talent and inspiration into such clan commissions, which have more cultural significance than cash income.

Following the Hoonah pieces, he made commissioned ceremonial art for other clans. As I see my father's work in ceremonial use today, I'm sure it will stand the test of time.

We will keep singing my uncles' songs. We will wear my mother's beadwork, which improves with time. My brothers and sisters all have her beadwork. She made pieces for all of us. My children, nieces and nephews, and grandchildren all have her works of art. She made beaded symbols for a vest for my husband, which he treasures. I'm also lucky to have one vest made with her creations. My mother has strung many glass beads and sewed beads throughout her life.

I am what I am from my family of artists and friends, from books and professional colleagues, and most important, from my husband and partner in my profession, Richard.

*Part Two*

POETRY

A POEM FOR JIM NAGATÁAK'W (JAKWTEEN)

*My Grandfather, Blind and Nearly Deaf*


I was telling my grandfather
about what was happening
on the boat. My father
and his brothers were trying to
anchor against the wind
and tide.

I could smell him, especially
his hair. It was a warm smell.
I yelled as loud as I could,
telling him what I saw.
My face was wet
from driving rain.

I could see his long eyebrows,
I could look at him and get
really close. We both liked this.
Getting close was his way
of seeing.

# GRANDPA JAKWTEEN IN ECLIPSE

He told his family
of when,
as a young man
hunting along a beach,
he was caught in a midday
eclipse of the sun.
According to Tlingit folk belief,
this could turn you
into a stone.
So he climbed up
on a high rock
where he could easily be seen.
(If he had to be a stone,
he wanted to be seen.)
Lucky for us,
he lived to tell the story.
No stone,
and his descendants
are like sand.

## AUNTIE FRANCES, MY FATHER'S SISTER

When her husband, Kendall,
bought her the first
wringer washing machine
in the family,
it was run by gas
and made a loud ruckus.
The entire house hummed
when she started her washing machine.
Keeping time
with its putt-putting,
feeding her wash and the wringer,
she looked as if she danced,
being twirled this way and that
by some invisible partner.

## MY AUNTIE JENNIE'S BED

She always slept on a bed
with many pillows,
small ones, large ones,
old and new.
Once in a while
she made me sit among them
and made me play rag dolls
with dolls made of old rags
from whatever she decided
was good for dolls.
My dolls always smelled
of raisins and seal oil
because I kept them
in a Sun Maid raisin box.
She helped me make the dolls
talk to each other.
On occasion
she had the dolls go fishing
or picking berries.
She gave each doll
a Tlingit name
and all the families had names as well.
She taught me how to give names
to Tlingit dolls.
I now give names to my grandchildren
and nieces and nephews.

## GRANDMOTHER ELIZA

My grandmother Eliza
was the family surgeon.
Her scalpel made from a pocketknife
she kept in a couple of pinches of snoose.
She saved my life by puncturing
my festering neck twice with her knife.
She saved my brother's life twice
when his arm turned bad.
The second time she saved him
was when his shoulder turned bad.
She always made sure
she didn't cut an artery.
She would feel around for days
finding the right spot to cut.
When a doctor found out
she saved my brother's life
he warned her,
"You know you could go to jail for this?"

Her intern, my Auntie Anny, saved my life
when I cut a vessel on my toe.
While my blood was squirting out
she went out into the night
and cut and chewed the bark
of plants she knew.
She put the granules of chewed up bark
on my toe before the eyes of the folks

who came to console my mother
because I was bleeding to death.
Grandma's other intern, Auntie Jennie,
saved our uncle's life when his son
shot him through the leg by accident.
A doctor warned her, too,
when he saw how she cured.
Her relative cured herself of diabetes.
Now, the doctors keep on asking,
"How did you cure yourself?"

## SALMON EGG PULLER—$2.15 AN HOUR

You learn to dance with machines,
keep time with the header.

Swing your arms,
reach inside the salmon cavity
with your left hand,
where the head was.

Grab lightly
top of egg sack
with fingers,
pull gently, but quick.
Reach in immediately with right hand
for the lower egg sack.
Pull this gently.

Slide them into a chute to catch the eggs.
Reach into the next salmon.
Do this four hours in the morning
with a fifteen minute coffee break.

Go home for lunch.
Attend to kids, and feed them.
Work four hours in the afternoon
with a fifteen minute coffee break.
Go home for dinner.
Attend to kids, and feed them.

Go back for two more hours,
four more hours.
Reach,
pull gently.

Go home for the day.
Attend to kids who missed you.
When fingers start swelling,
soak them in Epsom salts.
If you don't have time,
stand under a shower
with your hands up under the spray.
Get to bed early if you can.
Next morning, if your fingers are sore,
start dancing immediately.
The pain will go away
after icy fish with eggs.

IN MEMORY OF JEFF DAVID

*(Regional Basketball "All-American Hall of Famer")*


Even your name
proclaims it.
In Tlingit: S'ukḵées,
"Wolf Rib, Like a Bracelet,
Like a Hoop."
Scoring hook shots,
as center,
shooting from the key,
your body motion
forming a hoop
wolfing up the points.

## WILLIE

—In memory of my father, Willie Marks (1902–1981)


When I talked to you
in the hospital,
recovering from pneumonia,
you said to me,
you were ready to go.
"Don't worry, daughter,
I will be like X̱akúch' when the octopus
came up under him."
I was lost,
adrift on an ocean of tears
with no solid place
to beach my boat.

## MEMORIAL DAY IN KIEV

—for Lydia Black


The rain:
a mother's tears
for her children
falling on blossoms,

umbrellas
brightly colored
lining streets of Kiev
through steamy bus
and streetcar windows
from St. Sophia's
to cemetery,

and flowers
we carry for you
to your mother.

## TLINGIT ELDERS

Departed elders
of all the books we've done,
when I talk about you
all I feel is
pain
at your absence.

## MIGRATION CATALOG

Mental notes
of all the birds this spring:
three weeks left in March,
I saw brants on the Mendenhall tide flats;
two weeks left in March
I heard a Steller's jay
yakking away the day;
one week left in March,
I heard a robin;
one week into April,
geese flying high.
We made it once again.
Everything is fine.

SPRING

Skunk cabbage
punching through the ground,
punching to spring.

## BUDS

All of creation
is puckering with buds,
exploding their perfumes,
intoxicating all
who savor this aroma
of spring.

## BLOSSOMS

White, like fog:
blueberry blossoms
along the old Marks Trail,
each flower
a fragrant promise
of a fruitful season.

FROM CAMP HEAVEN

*A Letter to Chris, My Daughter-in-Law, Who Loves Flowers*

—for Chris


We climbed on Jacob's Ladders
leading up and up,
through Wild Crane's Bills
(geraniums), blue in a breeze,
over dovelike columbine,
lighting on tips of stems,
monks nodding in their hoods at us,
dolphins (delphiniums) surfacing here and there,
Day's Eyes (alpine daisies) gazing
over carpeting of saxifrage,
breaking rocks:
walking over
to Kelsall Lake, B.C.

## CONSTELLATION COURSE: HANGING LOOSE

*(Awaiting the Arrival of the Hawai'iloa Catamaran of the Polynesian Voyaging Society)*


Extreme anticipation.
You are like Love Medicine to all of us.
All the Tlingits of southeast Alaska
were as if in a tide pool,
churning,
when we heard, "The Hawai'ians are on their way!"
From Ketchikan
we heard word of you.
From Wrangell,
Petersburg,
Angoon,
Hoonah,
Haines:
all your ports of call.
When you were nearing Juneau,
as news of you grew stronger,
the tide rushed in full bore,
taking us along
on a current of
"Anxious to See You."
Symptoms of Love Medicine: smitten
helplessly,
waiting to see you,
anticipation
to da max.
Aloha!!

## TOTEMIC DISPLAY

*(Melt Creek, at the Confluence of the Alsek and Tatshenshini Rivers)*

No sooner had we landed
and climbed the riverbank, when
the huge brown bear stood,
a quivering mass of fur,
her cub quivering beside her:
my mother's beadwork,
shimmering glass facets
on a Brown Bear shirt.

# FOR MY GRANDDAUGHTERS GENNY AND LENNY

## *Jumping Rope with Ocean Breakers, Yakutat, Alaska*

Raven girls play
on the lip of Black Raven,
Genny jumping over each
arm of the foaming wing
sweeping in from under
the clouds.
Lenny screams, jumping away from
each wing-beat of froth.

Play, Genny, play,
play, Lenny, play.
This is your ancestors' beach.
Raven
pulled in the Salmon Box
at Dry Bay.
Play, Genny, play,
play, Lenny, play.
After pulling in the Salmon Box
he wiped his beak
along the Alsek River
at Alsek Lake, where rocks still fall.
Play, Genny, play,
play, Lenny, play.
Your ancestors' village
is in Kunaaġa.aa, Dry Bay.
Play, Genny, play,

play, Lenny, play.
Your ancestor Kuchein's
river flows over there,
Italio River.
Play, Genny, play,
play, Lenny, play.
Your river is the Alsek
we rafted down.
Play, Genny, play,
play, Lenny, play.
Your clan houses are still along that river,
where your great-grandmother
became Lukaax.ádi.
Play, Genny, play,
play, Lenny, play.
There's the bay where your ancestor Kaawus.aa
was given the name Dry Bay George.
Play, Genny, play,
play, Lenny, play.
Your ancestor George Frances
is in a grave
at Situk.
Play, Genny, play,
play, Lenny, play.
Grandma Kutkeinduteen,
the one before you,
is buried on Ankau (S'óos).
Play, Genny, play,
play, Lenny, play.
Aalséix, Alsek, is the river your ancestors
went over on glaciers to trade.
Play, Genny, play,
play, Lenny, play.
There are your ancestors
T'akdeintaan from Hoonah,
their Mount Fairweather Hat

your ancestor Willie carved.
Play, Genny, play,
play, Lenny, play.
For all of your family,
play, Genny, play,
play, Lenny, play.

## LETTER TO NANAO SAKAKI

I dance with
dancing cranes
(lilies of the valley),
transplanting them
under a tree until
next summer
when there will be
more dancers.

## ANGOON AT LOW TIDE

I know this smell:
of gumboots, chiton, shaaw;
of beach at minus tide,
warm with sun—
by any name,
a menu,
preparing for a feast.

## BERRIES

I could see
only the glare
of licorice jelly beans—
berries,
branches laden with
berries,
berries
for winter.

## CROSSING THE BRIDGE

I cross the bridge
as usual,
returning home,
panting from my pace.
Looking down,
I see four seals, the hunters,
frolicking
in the sea.
They dive,
and coming up,
one has a salmon
in its jaws.
The other two nearby
try stealing a bite.
The seal dives.
From the seaward shore
a regatta of red sockeye salmon,
in formation, on patrol,
crosses the channel.

## RAVEN AT GRAND CANYON

—for Joanne Townsend

All my senses are alive,
nerves jumping at the edge
from my toes to fingertips,
as they play tricks,
become Raven circling over me.
Every hair on my head
seems connected to him
ready to pull me over
from Maricopa Point
to Precambrian.

## COMING DOWN FROM THE MOGOLLON RIM

Where is there a place
to turn around?
Where are the guardrails
on the curves?
Looking down, my body
trembles to my lips,
feet pushing to the floorboard
as if to root,
to realize the long way down.
Even cactus cling, inclining,
sliding down.

## ZUNI RING: GLACIAL TURQUOISE

This turquoise ring,
a gift at Zuni,
takes me North again:
to glaciers at Alsek Lake,
the sky on clear day,
to my lover's eyes
when he looks at me,
the North Pacific Ocean
when the sun is setting
on the outer coast.

## FIELDWORK

Home,
with only your route
to look over.

It wasn't bad.
I read your itinerary,
followed you on the map
across Siberia, until
the places big enough to list
were gone.

It wasn't bad, but . . .

My! Nothing exciting. Only work.

Stayed awake, then went to Hoonah.
Ate breakfast with Ernestine.
Worked with her.

Ate crab with Katherine Mills.
Thought how you would love it.

Nothing but routine.

## ERNESTINE'S HOUSE, HOONAH, ALASKA, 6 A.M.

I woke to smell of smoke
of fresh wood crackling
from the stove,
bringing back the feel
of my father's clan house,
Brown Bear Den House
radiating families' care.
I can almost taste
the smoked deer meat
coming out of a container
of seal oil.
Brown Bear Den House—
a cavern of
memory.

## VARIATIONS OF TWO

I
The Yukon River
at minus three:
a tub of hot water drawn
for a morning bath.

II
A jet streaking northward
in the morning: a thermometer
rising on a blue wall.

III
The Yukon River
steams like a cauldron
in a horror movie.
The jet stream in the sky
is a thermometer
in some invisible hand
sinking, testing the brew.

## THE STORM

Like people
emerging from a steambath,
bending over,
steaming from their heads
and shoulders,
the ring of mountains
from the Chilkat Range
to the Juneau ice field
as if in steambath towels
of snow flurries;
at their feet
are foaming white caps of sea
like water thrown on rocks
steaming from the heat.

## STORMS FROM AN ENEMY SKY

(thinking of D'Arcy McNickle)


I feel storms
from an enemy sky.
A storm blows over us
and over everything else.
There is an undertow
created by an unknown force—
the politics of language—
turning my love
into a vile taste on my tongue.

## STEEL GRAY

The clouds are steel gray—
that cold look,
as if every piece of metal
is so cold your fingers could stick
if you touch them;
like a block of ice
when you touch with gloved hand
the gloves' fuzz is grabbed by the steel;
like the gray matter of thought:
everything sticks to it,
if you let it.

## TREES IN NORTH WIND

The trees
are coated with snow
as if robed in Chilkat blankets,
the wind—
a song,
as if led by a drumbeat.
The fringe of bottom branches
swirls around the trunks,
keeping time to the beat.
A wind rattle
blowing through the branches,
accompanies the drum.
This could be
a clan-house steward
with his grandchildren
making their debut,
brought out
to be recognized
and vested as descendants.

## AMELIA'S FIRST SKI RUN

*Eaglecrest, Juneau, February 24, 1989*

Amelia, space-age girl
at the top of Sourdough
makes her run with Eagle Grandpa Dick,
Raven girl, balancing on space,
gliding on air
in Tlingit colors:
black pants, turquoise jacket,
yellow shoulder patches,
black hair like feathers
clinging to her head,
face the color of red cedar.
Once in a while
I could even see space
between her legs and skis.
Diving downhill
she continues
side to side, slalom style,
following Grandpa's red boots.
Then the two figures swoop around the
corner,
swishing downhill,
shooshing home.

## TONIO SAVES CHRISTMAS

It was the day before Christmas
when Tonio was helping Grandma Nora
put up lights on her tiny tree.
They wouldn't light.
Tonio was like lightning
troubleshooting
each light.
In a couple of seconds he said,
"We need a bulb to make them blink too."
A few seconds later he said,
"There it is!"
He plugged it in,
smiling from ear to ear,
beaming.
We watched the little tree light up.

FOR MY GRANDDAUGHTER AMELIA

*Cheerleading at Homecoming '98, Juneau-Douglas High School*

Tears of pride fill
my eyes to the brim
shaping you into
a painting by Picasso,
gemlike, diamond-cut,
into one of his
sultry beauties.

*Part Three*

PLAYS

# *Introduction to the Raven Plays*

*I*n this section, I am very proud and happy to present three
Raven stories that I have adapted as stage plays from oral ver-
sions told in Tlingit by three of our storytellers.

Some people comment that they really don't look like plays at
all but are more like stories or storytelling. This is true. The plays
were commissioned by the Naa Kahidi Theater, a troupe originally
organized and sponsored by Sealaska Heritage Foundation, where
my husband and I worked for nearly fourteen years, developing the
program in Language and Cultural Studies. The theater specialized
in dramatizations of Tlingit stories. It began like most theaters,
with several actors having speaking parts. But it quickly evolved
into the concept of a single storyteller who delivers the narrative,
while other members of the cast act and dance in masks and costumes. This feature of writing and performance style brought the
theater closer to the traditional dramatic and ceremonial forms of
the Native people of the Northwest Coast and proved quite success-
ful and popular with audiences. It allowed for greater use of singing, drumming, dancing, and theatrical development of masks and
costumes. The storyteller also becomes a character, his or her personality interacting with the dancers. Working with elders in the
Tlingit community, David Hunsaker, the artistic director of the
theater, wrote several tragic pieces based on traditional narratives. I
was commissioned to write some comedy that would appeal to
children as well as adults.

For almost ten years, the Naa Kahidi Theater enjoyed enormous

Repartee between Storyteller (Gary Waid) and Raven (Gene Tagaban) in a
Naa Kahidi Theater production of *White Raven and Water*. (Courtesy of
the Naa Kahidi Theater)

popularity, playing at venues throughout the United States and in
Europe. These are worth mentioning. Beginning with Juneau and
southeast Alaska, the theater expanded into tours of the North-
west, playing at most major cities in Washington and Oregon.
Eventually, they played in all western states, including Hawaii, did a
Southwest tour, several eastern tours, and tours of the Midwest and
Canada. The Southwest tour involved a special staging combining
the tricksters Raven and Coyote. My plays have been performed in
the Kennedy Center in Washington, D.C., in the Cowell Theater in
San Francisco, in the Ordway Theater in Saint Paul, and at the Mu-

seum of the American Indian in New York City. The plays also toured Europe two or three times, playing in Spain, Italy, Switzerland, and the United Kingdom. The Naa Kahidi Theater was eliminated as part of the restructuring of Sealaska Heritage Foundation, but the plays continue to be performed by members of the original troupe and by their spin-off group, Yéil Sé, Raven's Voice Theater.

The Raven plays have always delighted audiences. Sometimes Raven confuses audiences, who worry if it's culturally appropriate or politically correct to laugh at Raven, who is rumored to be some kind of sacred figure. If this is so, he's some kind of sacred clown, and laughing is the whole idea. We laugh at Raven, and we laugh at ourselves. He is timeless and today. That's one reason I like to play with deliberate anachronisms and very contemporary language. Raven is the trickster figure in Tlingit literature and for many other people in Alaska and adjacent Canada. He plays the role that Coyote plays among many groups in the West and Southwest. Not technically a "creator," Raven is more an amoral rearranger and redistributor, shaping the world as we know it today, redistributing the resources, and making it more user-friendly for humans. We see this in the plays included here. Driven by hunger, greed, and lust, Raven is the ultimate con man, often using kinship terms and other co-membership strategies to smooth-talk his "marks" or victims. If humans benefit, it's usually by accident, as in *White Raven and Water*, where, in the course of his escape, Raven spills fresh water on the world. Using the "let's you and him fight" trick, Raven lures King Salmon to his death, and then tricks the small birds into helping him. They are lucky to escape alive, although the experience changes them forever. Raven almost loses in the adventure of his nose, but he manages to squeak through and fly away to another episode. Raven is a negative model. The stories warn us to beware of the Ravens we encounter every day but to be equally aware that a little bit of Raven lurks in each of us.

To avoid some potential confusion about the plays, I should say a word about one area of my life's work not included in this collection: the transcription and translation of Tlingit texts from oral tradition. The plays here are based on such stories by Tlingit elders but what is presented here is my own retelling. They are related to, but not the same as, the Raven stories told by Tlingit elders, in their own words, written down by me in Tlingit and published in facing translation. That work—in which I am the collector, scribe, translator, and, with my husband, co-editor—is being published by the University of Washington Press in an ongoing series called Classics of Tlingit Oral Literature. There are currently three volumes in print, and we are now working on a volume of Tlingit Raven stories. What's here is part of a new and expanding tradition of Native American literature composed in writing and in English but growing out of our general experience as Native people and our personal experience as individuals and members of family and community. Several wonderful elders, now departed, have given me or left me with these images and memories, and I want to help the stories continue by telling them again and by encouraging others to do so as well.

# White Raven and Water

## A Play Based on Tlingit Raven Stories Told by Willie Marks

WRITTEN FOR THE NAA KAHIDI THEATER

FIRST PERFORMED DURING THE 1993 SEASON

*Characters*
**Storyteller** (the only speaking role)
**Actors/dancers** wearing mask and wing constumes:
**Raven,** first in White, then Black
**Ganook,** a petrel

*Props*
bottles of soda
dog doo-doo in a tube (real or fake) or dog mess (real or fake)
water wheel made from roots
bentwood box water container
black gauze for the smoke

*Music*
Raven song, "Du yaa kanagoodi"

**Storyteller:**
White Raven,
walking along a beach:
He was looking for water.

He knew there was no water.
There was never any water anywhere
for people to drink,
but he thought he'd look anyway.
Only after it rained,
would people get to drink water.
But there was someone who was known to have water.
The one person who had water was Ganook.
Ganook lived out on Deikee Noow.
But Deikee Noow was waaaaaaay out there
on the Great Ocean.
He was Raven's brother-in-law
and the grandfather of the Alaska Native Birds.
Raven paced back and forth on the beach.
Every now and then
he looked out at Deikee Noow.
Raven: "How can I get out there?"
And then—
an idea!
Raven: "I think I'll go out there on a trip
to see my brother-in-law Ganook."
Raven flew waaaaay out there.
Nearly dead from dehydration,
Raven landed on Deikee Noow.
He was so weak he almost collided
with his brother-in-law.
He said to Ganook,
"Hey, Pardner! How are you?
I'm just out here on a small
vacation.
I asked for administrative leave.
I have a paid vacation,
but I didn't get any per diem.
Can I stay with you?"
Ganook hardly said a word.
He would do a "hrumf" once in a while.

Ganook defending his container of water from Raven in a Naa Kahidi
Theater production of *White Raven and Water*. (Courtesy of the Naa
Kahidi Theater)

In fact, he wouldn't talk to Raven at all.
Raven thought, "He has an attitude problem."
No matter what Raven said to him,
he didn't answer.
He stayed by his water.
He was preoccupied with his water.
All he did was sit on the lid of this marble container
for his water.
At times he would sit by the container,
but he never left it.
Once in a while he would stand by it
to stretch a little,
hanging on to the lid
just to make sure the lid of the water was on straight

and that no one bothered it.
Still thirsty, Raven thought,
"How can I get that water?"
He was sooooooo thirsty.
His mouth felt like it had a coat of glue inside.
He imagined Perrier in green bottles,
spritzers in all flavors,
Italian sodas,
birch beer, root beer, and Tumwater.
He wanted Ganook to get up from his water
and leave the marble container
so he could open the lid and have some.
He thought, "I must get the water."
An idea!!
While Ganook was asleep,
Raven brought in some dog doo-doo.
Holding the dog mess gingerly,
he smeared the bottom of Ganook with it.
Raven thought: "I hate to do this,
but—
I've just got to have some of that water."
The doo-doo smelled.
In fact, it was the smelliest smell ever.
Then he started to shake Ganook by his shoulder
to wake him from his sleep.
Raven turned his head away from the smell of the doo-doo.
Raven kept telling him,
"Hey! Hey! Hey! Hey!
Pardner! Pardner!
Wake up!
Hey! Wake up!"
Ganook slowly opened his eyes,
looking up at Raven.
Raven continued,
"You did something there!
It's all over your bottom

and it smells bad!
Yuck! Yuck! Yuck! Yuck!
Hey, Pardner,
you have to go out and clean yourself up!
You got a problem there!
It's gross!
I think you should go outside
and wipe it off!"
Ganook was sheepish and embarrassed.
Raven: "Pew! Yuck!"
Raven gagged at the smell.
This was when Ganook
went outside to wipe the doo-doo off.
Even he could hardly stand it.
He was gagging, too.
As soon as Ganook went out,
Raven, avoiding the smear on the lid,
grabbed the lid off the water
and threw it aside.
He stuck his head in
and with all his might,
glug, glug, glug, glug,
he gulped as much water as he could.
He swallowed the first of it.
Just picture skinny Raven
drinking all this water.
He was very skinny, you know.
While he was still gulping the water,
Ganook threw open the door,
yelling at Raven,
"Are you at it again?
Are you at it again?
Are you?
My precious water!
You never stop, do you?
You doo-doo butt Raven!"

At that, Raven flew out the smoke hole.
Gaa!
Ganook at the same instant yelled,
"Grab him, my Smoke Hole Spirit!
Grab him!"
The Spirit at the Smoke Hole
grabbed Raven.
Although he flapped his wings,
he couldn't move.
He flapped his wings in one place.
He kept on flapping there
at the smoke hole.
Then Ganook built a fire under him.
He used pitch-soaked wood
because it makes good smoke.
It was tough for Raven,
especially when the smoke was billowing up.
His eyes started to water.
His eyes were running,
and he wanted to sneeze
from the smoke.
He was inhaling smoke, and he wanted to cough so bad.
But he thought, "I've got to keep the water,
for my grandchildren."
Over the smoke hole
he flapped.
He kept on flapping.
He thought: "Oh! That smoke!
Won't he ever stop putting on the sapwood?"
He just flapped there.
The White Raven was flapping.
You know,
Raven was white
before Ganook's fire.
He was originally white.
He had the water in his mouth

and inside of him.
He held it in his mouth with all his might
while he was flying at the smoke hole.
It was very difficult to hold the water.
His eyes were bulging from the pressure.
It was tough for him.
But it was for all the people
and for the world
so that everyone and all the animals
could drink fresh water.
Ganook continued to smoke him.
He piled his wood on high.
Only after Raven was so black,
like a hunk of coal,
Ganook said,
"Spirit Over My Fire,
let Raven go,
let him go."
With the last of his strength
he flew away,
looking like a little hunk of coal
in the air.
By this time
he could hardly hold the water
in his mouth.
He thought, "I'll try to hold the water
even if some of it dribbles."
He dribbled from his beak.
These dribbles
from the corners of his beak
made the streams in southeast Alaska.
This is what became the streams.
An idea!
"I'll spit some out!" he thought.
Maybe the water he spit out
made the first rivers,

the huge rivers coming down from the north:
the Yukon,
Copper,
Alsek,
Chilkat,
Taku,
Sitkine,
and the Nass.
But when he was naming them,
who wrote it all down?
Was there someone there
with a pencil and pad
to transcribe his story?
Anyway,
this is how
Raven spit out the rivers
by mouthfuls
throughout the world.
Then he designed the waterfalls,
the falls that don't have lakes at their head.
Even today you can see the waterfalls
pouring from the mountains.
Raven thought, "How shall I design the falls?"
An idea!
He gathered the mountain ferns
called Shaa Luka Leet'i in Tlingit.
Then he wove them
into a wheel.
While he was spinning it like a wheel,
he spit water on it
as it turned.
He spit out the water
that he still had left in his mouth.
After he spit the water onto the wheel,
he rolled the wheel holding the water
over the side of the mountain.

The wheel released the water
as it fell.
This is how Raven made the waterfalls
on the mountainsides.
This water flows in a circle.
That's why it never runs out.
This is how we got water in the world,
and this is how Raven invented
the hydrogen cycle.
Raven was so hungry
after getting all the water in place
that he started
walking along the beach,
looking for something to eat,
thinking,
"Who shall I go see next?"
He flew away.
Gaa! Gaa!
[Exit, with Raven Song, "Du yaa kanagoodi"]

# Raven, King Salmon, and the Birds

## A Play Based on Raven Stories by Katherine Mills and George Davis

WRITTEN FOR NAA KAHIDI THEATER

FIRST PERFORMED DURING THE FALL 1989 SEASON

JUNEAU; WASHINGTON, D.C.; AND OREGON

*Characters*
**Storyteller** (the only speaking role except for "chorus" phrase
     spoken by the entire cast)
**Actors/dancers** wearing mask and wing costumes:
**Raven**
**Robin**
**Chickadee**
**Blue Jay**
**Magpie**

*Props*
plastic club or long balloon
stump
greenstone
skunk cabbage leaves
salmon (may be either a prop or dancer)

*Music*
Raven Song, "Du Yaa Kanagoodi"

SCENE I
A BEACH IN SOUTHEAST ALASKA


**Storyteller:**
Raven: walking along a beach.
He sees a King Salmon
jumping out of the water.

> **Chorus** [as Salmon jumps]:
> *Ei haaw! Ei haaw! Ei haaw! Ei haaw!*

He stared and stared,
hungrily.
Raven hadn't eaten for days.
He could hear his stomach growling.
[Raven makes sound of stomach rumble]
He could almost taste the salmon.
He thought,
"How could I get the salmon
to come in?"
Then he found a Greenstone.
He brushed it off
and turned it this way and that way.
An idea!
"I'll put this up on a stump!"
Then Raven said,
"Hey, you! You dirty guy!
Listen to what this Greenstone
is saying about you.
Hey, you!
Listen to what he's saying!"

> **Chorus:**
> *Ei haaw! Ei haaw! Ei haaw! Ei haaw!*

King Salmon jumped out there.
Raven yelled at the Salmon,
"Hey, you!
Listen to what this little green stone
is saying about you.
Listen!"
King Salmon jumped out there,
out from the beach Raven was on.

    **Chorus:**
      *Ei haaw! Ei haaw! Ei haaw! Ei haaw!*

Raven starts yelling insults.
"Hey, you!
Listen to what Greenstone said.
Come on ashore!
Come, jump on the beach!"

    **Chorus:**
      *Ei haaw! Ei haaw! Ei haaw! Ei haaw!*

And King Salmon
jumped up on the beach.
Raven,
in his foolishness
and shortsighted exploit,
forgot he should have had a club
to hit the nose
of the King Salmon.
So he told the King Salmon,
"Oh, my! Pardner,
let me go in the woods first.
I can hardly stand it!"
So he ran up in the woods
to get a club.
When he came back down,

he had his club.
But the King Salmon
was out in the bay again,
jumping around.

> **Chorus:**
> *Ei haaw! Ei haaw! Ei haaw! Ei haaw!*

He jumped out there.
Raven: "Hey!
Listen to what the Greenstone
is saying about you!
You dirty mouth!
You dirty-gilled person, you!
Hey! Do you hear this?"
Salmon jumped out there,
not bothered.

> **Chorus:**
> *Ei haaw! Ei haaw! Ei haaw! Ei haaw!*

Raven: "Here's what he just said.
You dirty spined salmon."
At this the salmon
jumped on the beach
by Raven.
As it jumped on the beach
Raven attacked it
with the club.
He slammed the club on its nose
again and again and again and again
until it was gone.

## SCENE II
## FARTHER UP THE BEACH, ABOVE THE TIDELINE

**Storyteller:**
The salmon was too heavy for him,
so Raven organized
a group of birds
called Alaska Native Birds.
Their acronym
is ANB.
Raven said to them,
"Hey, Grandchildren.
Help me pull this salmon up,
and we'll bake it."
When they pulled it up, Raven said,
"We have to dig a pit for the salmon."
They dug a huge pit.
Then Raven said, "Gee!
Now we gotta get some skunk cabbage
to wrap our salmon with,
and so we can put some skunk cabbage
on the bottom of the fire pit.
Why don't you go and get some?"
Birds: "Let's pick only the nice ones.
That guy is a nice guy."
They went and picked nice huge ones,
nice clean ones,
and hurried back with them.
Then Raven asked them,
"Let me see."
They piled them up in front of him.
Then he looked them over.
While he looked them over
he asked,
"Where did you pick them?"

They all pointed to the same place
behind the village.
Raven exploded,
"Yuck! Yuck! Yuck! Yuck!
It's contaminated there!
It's as bad as PCBs.
When my wife was alive
she used to go over there!
Throw them away!
They're not fit
to wrap the salmon in!
Throw them away!
Throw them away!
Look at the brown spots on them!"
He was pointing to imaginary spots on them.
The little birds were sad,
but they still wanted to help Raven.
Birds: "We'll get better ones,
and clean ones too."
Raven told them,
"Go over two mountains.
Get the skunk cabbage
only from there."
Birds: "How could we know
that his wife used to go there?
We should have asked."
They left.
Birds: "Let's hurry.
Salmon is fresh
for only a while."
They hiked.
In the meantime
Raven put the layers of skunk cabbage
and the salmon over them
on the bottom of the pit
the birds had dug for him.

He covered it
and built a fire over it.
When it was done
Raven ate
to his heart's content.
Once in a while
he would burp a long one.
You see,
it's okay to burp
at a Tlingit dinner.
So he ate and ate
and burped and burped
until he ate up
the whole salmon
("Oops! I ate it all!")
before the birds could have any.
He was content.
All that was left was the tail.
He put his craft to work.
He tried to roll a stump
over the fire.
He couldn't.
So he finally just stuck
the tail under it.
He said,
"There!"
When the birds came back
Raven was sitting
by the uprooted tree stump
looking sad, and saying,
"We're so unlucky, you guys!
This tree stump
rolled over on the salmon
on the fire
and we can't even salvage

any of it!
We've lost all of it!
It's all gone!
All the skunk cabbage
were brought for nothing."
Only the tail
was sticking out
from under the stump.
The birds were sad.
They cried.
The birds were wailing.
All the birds were crying
"Waaaaaaaa!"
Some were angry.
Raven was in a fix.
He thought,
"What am I going to do?"
An idea!
Raven: "Hey! You guys!
Why are you crying?
Come here!"
Robin came over.
Robin was cold
and got too close to the fire.
When her belly caught fire
she didn't even feel it
until it was red.
Robin: "Ouch! I'm burning!"
Chickadee was crying.
She rubbed her eyes.
She was so upset while she cried
she rubbed her eyes
and the top of her head.
She rubbed in the soot
she had all over her

from the ashes she was sitting in.
"I'm tired and hungry," she said.
Blue Jay was so angry he went on,
"Yakidi, yakidi, yakidi, yakidi, yak!
You should have cooked the salmon
more carefully!
You should not have built
the fire there
near the stump!"
Raven pulled Blue Jay's feathers
around his head
into a topknot
or a bow.
Raven: "You shouldn't be squawking!
Look at what a nice-looking guy you are!
You look funny angry!"
Magpie was trying to fly off,
but Raven pulled him back
and tried to calm him down
by running his claws
down his tail.
That's why Magpie
has that long tail.
This is where Chickadee
got her black top
and black rings around the eyes.
Robin burned her belly
trying to get at the fire.
Blue Jay still has the comb
Raven made for him
and is still angry
he didn't get any salmon.
What happened to Raven?
After he smooth-talked
the Alaska Native Birds,

he realized he had been so busy for so long
he'd worked up an appetite.
You could hear his stomach growling.

**Chorus:**
*Growwwwlllllllll!*

He quickly grabbed
the King Salmon tail, and said,
"I think I'll go see
my brother-in-law, the Brown Bear.
And he flew away.

**Chorus:**
*[Sings Raven song, "Du yaa kanagoodi"]*

# Raven Loses His Nose

## A Play Based on a Story Told by Susie James

WRITTEN FOR THE ACTORS OF NAA KAHIDI THEATER
AND YÉIL SÉ, RAVEN'S VOICE THEATER

*Characters*
**Storyteller** (the only speaking role)
**Raven**
**fishermen**
**townspeople**
**museum guard**

*Props*
fishing bait, real or fake
detachable Raven beak
pine cone
white museum gloves

*Music*
Raven song, "Du yaa kanagoodi"

**Storyteller:**
Raven—walking along a beach.
He's hungry again.
He's always hungry.
No matter what he eats,
he's never satisfied.

He's always looking for something else to eat.
(Aside: Maybe he eats Chinese food,
this is why he's always hungry.)
His stomach is growling.
[Growl]
Raven: "I wish i had some of that salmon now
that my grandchildren and I
baked on the beach.
It was sooooooo tasty!"
He keeps on looking for something to eat.
"Where can I get something to eat?"
He keeps on going along the beach.
He's having hunger pangs.
His stomach keeps on growling.
[Growl]
He's starting to hallucinate.
At first about salmon,
and herring,
and any kind of fish
he might encounter on the beach.
And then his hallucinations change
to Golden Arches and Big Macs
and Taco Bell.
Even a crispy morsel would be good
from the old man in white who sells
buckets of deep-fried birds.
Maybe even a bite or two from Pizza Hut.
He's even salivating
over Jack-in-the-Box.
As he walks along the beach
he staggers from side to side from hunger.
He thinks about the parking lots of grocery stores
where he can always pick up an Oreo cookie
or a slice of bread,
or maybe a Hostess Twinkie
(but he's gotta watch his weight).

His mouth waters at the thought of this, too.
Drifting out of his hallucination,
he keeps on walking.
As he walks, he comes on this village
where people are getting ready
to go out jigging for halibut.
He tries to beg from the fishermen
carrying bait down to their boats.
Raven: "Say, you guys.
Could I have some of the fat from your tray of bait?"
"Hey, Buddy. Take a number and get in line!"
Raven can taste the flavor.
He starts pacing back and forth.
"How can I get some of those goodies?"
Those nice morsels of bait:
seal fat, the kind you can chew like bubble gum.
Raven, smacking his lips, can taste the fat.
But he seems invisible to the fishermen.
They just ignore him.
(Aside: Have you ever felt like that in a store?
Raven felt terrible.
But even this didn't damage
his self-esteem.)
An idea!
"Maybe I can go down to the bottom of the sea,
where they lower the bait!"
He looks around and decides
it's too open by the village.
There are too many people
who can see what he's doing.
(Raven, aside: "I wish I'd brought my nephew's
Aqua-Lung and flippers.")
He looks for the ideal place
to enter under the sea.
At last he finds a spot
where no one can see him.

He finds two giant boulders
with space in between them.
"This looks as good a place as any."
He tries to lift the sea.
It seems to be stuck to the beach.
He can't lift it like he thought he could.
He starts checking other spots along the beach.
He finally comes on a place
where the ocean is loose but not too watery,
where he can lift the edge
and get down under the sea.
When he gets down there and looks
to see why the ocean was stuck,
he sees a bunch of chitons giggling,
trying to keep from laughing out loud at him.
They were the creatures
holding down the sea
when he tried to lift it
to get under.
As he's going down he thinks again,
"I really wish I'd brought
my nephew's scuba diving gear,
especially those flippers."
Far off he can see the fishing lines
with baited hooks dangling
near the bottom of the sea.
At times they look like they're swimming along, like fish.
Raven tiptoes over there, salivating,
heading for the hooks,
with bait on them.
He's salivating so much now
it's making the sea cloudy and bubbly.
(Raven, aside: "I'm glad they're not hoochies
because hoochies are plastic.
They're no good for eating,
and they're no good for the environment.

They're not biodegradable.")
When he gets there he uses his very lightest touch
to unhook the bait.
As he unhooks each piece
he tosses the bait in his mouth
and gulps it down without chewing.
Each time he unhooks the bait, he swallows it.
Then he tugs on the hook,
like a fish biting.
Up above in the boats,
the fishermen are confused.
They say, "Daa sáyá? What's this?"
They've never seen anything like it.
They've got so many bites but no fish.
They send for a consultant,
a bite expert,
to tell them what kind of bites they're feeling.
On feeling the first bite, he says, "It's a strange being."
Then at one point
Raven gets too greedy and careless
trying to cram so much seal fat
into his mouth all at once.
He pops the bait in his mouth
with a hook still on it.
As the hook goes through his beak, he jumps around.
He tries to say, "Ouch! Ouch! Ouch! Ouch!"
But water just pours into his mouth
and he starts to gurgle and gargle.
The fishermen on the boat above
give a big yank with their fiberglass poles,
with their Penn reel and line,
to set the hook.
They hold on tight so the fish won't get away.
"We can't lose this one," they say.
(Aside: "They're kneeling in the bottom of the boat.
But, did you ever notice how the white folks

Raven with his long beak, from a 1989 Naa Kahidi Theater production. (Photograph by Pacific Communications; courtesy of the Naa Kahidi Theater)

always stand up in the boat
when they get a strike?")
As the fishermen set the hook,
Raven's nose is yanked along.
He tries to pull free.
Raven is in deep trouble.
He shakes his head from side to side.
On the surface it feels to the fishermen
like a fish trying to get loose.
They're getting very excited.
Raven tries yanking his beak free.
The fishermen think they've hooked on to something big.
They're very happy and excited.
"At tlein áyá.
This is a biggie," they say.
They begin pulling it up slowly.
Raven is still on the ocean floor
trying to yank out the hook,
jumping this way and that.
The more he tries, the deeper he's hooked.
He pulls and he pulls and he yanks and he yanks.
No way can he get it out.
And then he shakes his head.
He can't get loose.
As he's being pulled up, he says,
"Oh! Oh! They're pulling me up."
By this time he's so exhausted
his wings just go limp and open up,
so the fishermen pulling him up
think he's a huge fish.
They say to each other, "This is really a big one.
I hope the line doesn't break."
"No! It's my new Penn reel
and my new monofilament
100-pound-test line
from K-Mart."

The line is taut.
It's about ready to break.
With his wings open, his belly side up,
Raven is gliding far out, then back, zigzagging.
When he does this the fishermen are convinced
he's a giant fish running all over.
"Aan yaa naltsís!!! Yoox̱ iltsées!!" they say.
"He's running with the line! Stopping,
then taking off again!"
When they pull him up near to the bottom of the boat,
when Raven gets this close,
he quickly glides under the boat
and puts his claws
on the bottom of the boat
resisting the pull of the fishermen.
The fishermen pull and pull.
Raven's in deep doo-doo.
He's holding the hook and the line with his hands,
his feet up under the boat, pushing away.
Then a bunch of fishermen pull and pull together
and they yank his nose clean off.
When they get his nose aboard they ask, "What is it?
It's not a fish."
One of them says, "I've never seen anything like it."
They can't figure out what it is,
so they say, "Send for our consultant.
He knows about a lot of things.
He's an expert at this.
Maybe we can sell it
to the Museum of Natural History.
But we need an appraisal first."
Someone runs to get the consultant.
Raven, in the meantime, can hear them talking.
He wades back to shore,
trying to cover his face
and his missing nose.

Raven: "I've just gotta get my nose back!"
An idea!
"My sister-in-law told me about this new law
for getting things back from museums.
It's called repatriation.
Maybe I can get my nose repatriated
to its indigenous owner.
Maybe it's an object
of cultural patrimony."
Raven, in his resourcefulness,
disguises himself as the consultant.
But he doesn't have a nose.
So as he walks like the consultant to examine his beak,
he sees a pine cone.
He puts some pitch on it
and sticks it on his face in place of his beak.
He pulls his hat, which is a limpet shell, down over his face.
Then he goes to see about his beak.
When he gets to the village
he goes to the first house and knocks.
Someone inside answers, "Yeah?"
He asks about the object.
"I'm the consultant," he says.
People tell him,
"It's next door."
When he gets to the next house and knocks,
somebody hollers, "Yeah?"
He asks again,
but they also tell him, "Go next door."
I guess they're giving him
the bureaucratic runaround.
After many houses,
he finds the place at last
where Raven's beak is being kept.
There's a person watching over the beak,
which is now on special exhibit.

When he asks to see it, this person tells him,
"First, you need an ID tag.
You can get one over there at the front desk."
So, Raven gets an ID tag.
Then they tell him,
"You also need to wear
these special gloves."
They give him a pair of white, gauzelike gloves.
Then he approaches his beak very slowly,
with appropriate reverence and awe.
It's resting on display
on a pile of down feathers
on a pedestal
under a special light.
As the guard goes with him to look at it,
Raven can see at once it's his beak,
but he solemnly reports to the guard,
"We call this Gunéit Loowú—An Alien's Beak.
I must examine it more closely."
So the guard lets him pick it up
so he can take a closer look at it.
He looks at it this way and that,
turning it over and over,
viewing it very carefully from all sides and angles.
While he's looking it over with one hand,
he can easily pull his pine cone beak free with the other.
One moment the beak's in his hand,
the next it's in place on his face.
In a flash
he tosses the pine cone aside
and flies out the smoke hole.
"Gaa!!"
When they see him do this they yell after him,
"Doo-doo butt Raven!"
Gaa! Gaa!
[Exit, with Raven song, "Du yaa kanagoodi"]

# Glossary

**Alaska Native Brotherhood** (ANB). A social and political organization founded in 1912. The Brotherhood fought for citizenship, voting rights, integration, land claims, and other civil rights issues. It is the oldest Native American organization in the United States.

**bentwood box.** A container for which Northwest Coast cultures are famous, made by steaming and bending a single piece of wood into the four sides of a box, the sides and lid of which are typically elaborately carved and painted.

**chitons.** Mollusks that live on the underside of rocks and are harvested at low tide. The giant chiton (*Cryptochiton stelleri*) is the most commonly eaten, either pickled, in chowder, or fried in patties. The smaller specimens are popularly called "gumboot," and the larger are called "Chinese slippers." The Tlingit word for chiton is shaaw.

**dryfish.** Fish that has been thinly sliced and dried in a smokehouse. The smoke flavors the fish as it desiccates and keeps flies away. There are various stages of drying, and the fish are then stored and eaten accordingly—eaten dry, boiled with potatoes, etc. Halibut, hooligan, black cod, and various species of salmon are commonly dried.

*Ei haaw.* An expression or cry used by Tlingit fishermen of southeast Alaska to signal a fish jumping. It is quicker to say "Ei haaw" than to say "Look! There's a fish jumping over there!"

**fish camp.** A seasonal camp set up close to the resource, where a family or community gathers to process and preserve fish for the winter.

**Gaa.** Raven's cry, "Caw."

**girdy.** A mechanized pulley to raise and lower fishing lines on a large troller.

**gumboot.** *See* chiton.

**Hall of Famer.** A man who is recognized for his career performance in local and regional amateur basketball, analogous to the Major League Baseball Hall of Fame, but the Tlingit hall of fame has no building or central archives.

**hoochies.** Imitation squidlike fishing bait made of soft rubber.

**jigging.** A fishing technique usually used when the objective is bottom fish, such as halibut, which lie on the sea floor. Jigging involves lowering a hook and line, with or without a pole, to the bottom and giving it a tug from time to time. This technique is in contrast to casting the line and reeling it in, and trolling. *See also* trolling.

**k'ínk'.** Fermented fish heads traditionally prepared in a pit on the beach that is regularly irrigated by tidal action.

**potlatch.** The main ceremonial event in Tlingit and other traditional Northwest Coast spirituality and folklife. Typically performed as a memorial for a departed clansperson, people of the departed's clan invite clans of the opposite moiety to assist in the removal of grief. The host clan distributes food, blankets, and other gifts to the guests.

**sealing boat.** A double-ended rowboat with two sets of oarlocks. Used for hunting seal and for hand trolling.

**seining.** A common method of commercial fishing on the Northwest Coast. A net with a floating cork line on the top and a lead-weighted line on the bottom is set out in a circle and then drawn together like a purse as the lines are pulled on board either by hand or by a pulley called a power block.

**shaaw.** The Tlingit word for chiton.

**skunk cabbage (*Lysichitum americanum*).** Common to swampy areas all along the Northwest Coast, this is a large plant, with leaves often more than a yard tall. It has a bright yellow spike and hood blossom early in the spring. It is popularly called "Indian wax paper" because it has many of the same uses. One traditional use is to line pits for steaming food.

**Snoose.** Snuff; pulverized tobacco.

**trolling.** A fishing technique that involves trailing one or more lines behind a moving boat. The girl rowing the "Egg Boat" uses hand trolling, a traditional method that involves holding on to the line and activating the lure by the act of rowing. Most small commercial fishermen run four separate standard poles on their powerboats, or two heavier poles of wood or metal, with several lines trailing from each. Sport fishermen can run one pole per licensed fisherman on board.

**X̲akúch'.** One of the legendary ancestors of my father's clan, the Chookaneidí, of the Eagle moiety, of Hoonah, who lost his life doing battle with a giant octopus not too far from what is now the entrance to Glacier Bay.

# Acknowledgments

"Entering the Salmon Stream," "Trolling," and "Dryfish Camp" were written for and first published in *First Fish, First People: Salmon Tales of the North Pacific Rim,* edited by Judith Roche and Meg McHutchison (Seattle: One Reel and the University of Washington Press, 1998). "Egg Boat" was first published in *Neek: News of the Native Community,* (Sitka, Alaska), edited by Andrew Hope III, vol. 1, no. 2 (January 1980). "Life Woven with Song" was written for *Here First: Autobiographical Essays by Native American Writers,* edited by Brian Swann and Arnold Krupat (New York: Random House/Modern Library, 2000). "Grandmother Eliza" first appeared in *Rolling Stock* (Boulder, Colorado), no. 19/20 (1991). "Memorial Day in Kiev" and "My Auntie Jennie's Bed" first appeared in *From the Island's Edge: A Sitka Reader,* edited by Carolyn Servid (Saint Paul, Minn., Graywolf Press, 1995). "For My Granddaughters Genny and Lenny" first appeared in the *Northern Review* (Yukon College, Whitehorse, Alaska), special literary issue, edited by Eric Heyne, no. 10 (Summer 1993). "Ernestine's House," "Raven at Grand Canyon" (under the title "At Grand Canyon II"), and "Totemic Display" first appeared in *Returning the Gift: Poetry and Prose from the First North American Native Writers' Festival,* edited by Joseph Bruchac (Tucson: University of Arizona Press, 1994). "Variations of Two," "In Memory of Jeff David," "Spring," "Willie," "Poem for Jim Nagatáak'w," and "Salmon Egg Puller" first appeared in the *Wicazo Sa Review: A Journal of Indian Studies* (Cheney, Washington), special issue on poetry from Alaska, edited by James Ruppert, vol. 5, no. 1 (Spring 1989). *Raven, King Salmon, and the Birds* was first published in *Raven Tells Stories: An Anthology of Alaskan Native Writing,* edited by Joseph Bruchac (Greenfield Center, N.Y.: Greenfield Review Press, 1991).

# *About the Author*

Nora Marks Dauenhauer was born in Juneau, Alaska, in 1927 and was raised in Juneau and Hoonah, as well as on the family fishing boat and in seasonal fishing, hunting, and trapping sites around Icy Strait, Glacier Bay, and Cape Spencer. Her first language is Tlingit; she began to learn English when she entered school at the age of eight. She has a bachelor's degree in anthropology from Alaska Methodist University and is internationally recognized for her fieldwork in and transcription, translation, and explication of Tlingit oral literature. In 1980 she was named Humanist of the Year by the Alaska Humanities Forum. In 1989 she received an Alaska Governor's Award for the Arts, and in 1991 she was a winner of the Before Columbus Foundation's American Book Award. From 1983 to 1997 she was principal researcher in language and cultural studies at Sealaska Heritage Foundation in Juneau. In addition to her folklore work, her creative and expository writing has been widely published and anthologized. Her first collection of poetry was *The Droning Shaman*, published in 1988 by Black Current Press. She is married to Richard Dauenhauer, writer and former poet laureate of Alaska. She has four children, thirteen grandchildren, and twelve great-grandchildren.